Ar K 9509

Queen Eleanor

Queen Eleanor

Independent Spirit
of the Medieval World

A biography of Eleanor of Aquitaine

Polly Schoyer Brooks

Houghton Mifflin Company
Boston

Library of Congress Cataloging-in-Publication Data
Brooks, Polly Schoyer.
Queen Eleanor, independent spirit of the medieval world.
Summary: A biography of the twelfth-century queen—first of
France, then of England—who was the wife of Henry II and
mother of several notable sons, including Richard the
Lionhearted.
ISBN 0-395-98139-5
1. Eleanor, Queen, consort of Henry II, King of England,
1122?–1204—Juvenile literature. 2. Great Britain—Queens—
Biography— Juvenile literature. 3. France—Queens—
Biography—Juvenile literature. [1. Eleanor, Queen, consort of
Henry II, King of England, 1122?–1204. 2. Kings, queens, rulers,
etc.] I. Title.
DA209.E6B76   1983
942.03'1'0924 [B][92]   82-48776

Printed in the United States of America
QUM 10 9 8 7 6 5 4

To my four lovely granddaughters,
Rebecca, Catherine, Abigail, Rosemary

Acknowledgments

The author wishes to thank her husband, Ernest Brooks, for his invaluable help and support throughout the writing of this book.

Thanks also to the following for permission to quote passages from their publications:

From *Eleanor of Aquitaine* by Regine Pernoud. Copyright © 1967 by Regine Pernoud. Used by permission of Coward-McCann, Inc., a division of Penguin Putnam Inc.

From *Eleanor and the Four Kings* by Amy Kelly. Copyright © 1950 by the President and Fellows of Harvard College. Reprinted by permission of Harvard University Press.

Acknowledgment is made to the following sources for the pictures appearing on the pages noted:

Archives Photographique C.N.M.H.S., Paris, France, page 165.

Bibliothèque Nationale, Paris, France, cliché Bibliothèque nationale de France, pages 20 and 38.

Bodleian Library, Oxford, England: Ms. Douce 208, folio 120 verso. Miniature, page 75.

By permission of the British Library, London, England, pages 15, 49, 57, 86–87, and 103.

The Master and Fellows of Corpus Christi College, Cambridge, England, page 128.

French Government Tourist Office, New York, N.Y., pages 5 and 161.

Heidelberg University Library, Heidelberg, Germany, pages 68, 78, and 111.

The Metropolitan Museum of Art, New York, N.Y., The Cloisters Collection, 1934, page 64.

The Metropolitan Museum of Art, New York, N.Y., Gift of J. Pierpont Morgan, 1917, page 69.

Museum of Fine Arts, Boston, Mass., Gift of Mr. & Mrs. Alastair Bradley Martin, page 158.

Picture Collection, The Branch Libraries, The New York Public Library, New York, N.Y., pages 28, 117, and 142.

Pierpont Morgan Library/Art Resource, New York, N.Y., pages 6, 88, and 109.

Walters Art Gallery, Baltimore, Md., page 94.

Contents

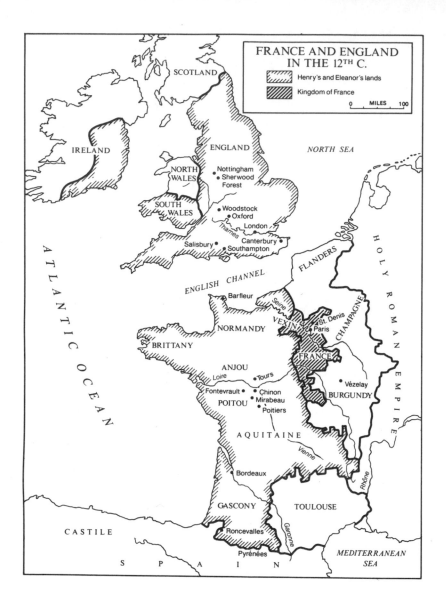

FRANCE AND ENGLAND
IN THE 12TH C.

Henry's and Eleanor's lands

Kingdom of France

0   MILES   100

SCOTLAND

IRELAND

ENGLAND

NORTH SEA

NORTH
WALES

Nottingham
Sherwood
Forest

SOUTH
WALES

Woodstock
Oxford

Thames

London

Salisbury
Southampton

Canterbury

ENGLISH CHANNEL

FLANDERS

HOLY ROMAN EMPIRE

ATLANTIC OCEAN

Barfleur

Seine

NORMANDY

VEXIN

St. Denis
Paris

CHAMPAGNE

BRITTANY

ANJOU

Loire

Tours

FRANCE

Fontevrault

Chinon
Mirabeau

Vézelay

BURGUNDY

POITOU

Poitiers

AQUITAINE

Vienne

Bordeaux

Rhône

GASCONY

TOULOUSE

CASTILE

Roncevalles

Garonne

Pyrénées

S   P   A   I   N

MEDITERRANEAN
SEA

Introduction

Eleanor and the Twelfth Century

For the first time in over two hundred years the great Duchy of Aquitaine was without a male heir. The long line of Duke Williams came abruptly to an end in 1137, when the tenth Duke William died, leaving his vast landholdings, one quarter the extent of modern France, to his young daughter Eleanor.

This book is the story of Eleanor's life, which spans most of the twelfth century, the very peak of the Middle Ages. Though it was a time when women had no equal rights and little or no power, Eleanor became one of the most influential leaders and was involved in all the great events of her era. She was the key figure in an endless quarrel between the

French and English kings. At times she ruled like a king herself and dealt with emperors and popes. More important, she won respect for women and made gentlemen of crude warrior knights. Her independent, outspoken nature made enemies among conservatives who did their best to blacken her reputation. But Eleanor had the courage to uphold her convictions.

Eleanor could trace her ancestors back to the time of Charlemagne, the Emperor who had united western Europe under one strong government three centuries earlier. Charlemagne had brought order out of the chaos of the Dark Ages that had enveloped Europe since the collapse of the Roman Empire and the wild confusion set in motion by wave after wave of barbarian invasions. Unfortunately, Charlemagne's great empire did not long survive his death. Under his weak descendants, it broke up into a jumble of little kingdoms, duchies, and counties. New invaders—Huns from the east, Moslems from the south, and the terrifying Viking pirates from the north—took advantage of these weak states and plunged the west once more into anarchy. Charlemagne's civilizing progress was set back as lawlessness and fighting became the order of the day. The most destructive invaders of all, the Vikings, looted and killed without mercy; they spared neither church nor monastery, neither women nor children. "From the fury of the Northmen, deliver us, oh Lord," prayed the terrified people. Many believed the dire prediction that the world was coming to an end in precisely the year 1000. But the year 1000 came and went and the world was still here. The invasions gradually abated; by the eleventh century Europe was well on the road to recovery. The Northmen had become farmers and settled in Normandy; the Huns had been driven east; the Moslems in Spain, known as Moors, had begun to spread their highly developed culture to the Spanish Christians.

When Eleanor was born in 1122, new forces for a more civilized way of life had begun to stir. Though there was still no unified government in western Europe, there was one bond that united society: the Christian faith. Almost everyone was a Catholic. Christian fervor was at its height and was to inspire a whole new church architecture, the soaring Gothic cathedral, built to the glory of God. Men and women went on long pilgrimages to distant shrines of saints and holy martyrs. Christianity also inspired the mail-clad knights—constantly fighting each other to get more land, or to keep what land they had, or just for sport—to unite as soldiers of the Lord and wage so-called holy wars, or crusades, against the Moslems. While the crusades did little for the Christian cause, they did open up trade with the wealthy Near East, and contact with the more civilized and educated Moslems aroused a new interest in learning, the arts, and a taste for luxury among the western Christians. The West shook off its semibarbaric past and began to live in a little more comfort and refinement. Scholars traveled long distances to find teachers and books. People outside the church began to read. Lyric poetry and romances about King Arthur expressed new ideals of chivalry. In all these beginnings Eleanor played an important part.

As we live in a democratic society, Eleanor lived in what is called a feudal society. Though feudalism had begun in the Dark Ages before Charlemagne, it quickened and widened its grip on society after the breakup of his empire, during the new invasions when people thought only of their own security. Kings were too weak to defend their little kingdoms, and the fear-stricken people sought protection from the nearest strong man. A nearby armed knight was more useful than a faraway weak king. Peasants flocked to the nearest local lord and took refuge in his stronghold, willingly surrendering their freedom and promising to provide their lord with a share of crops and other necessities of life in exchange for protection. This contract between the weak and the strong was the basis of the feudal system under which people lived for centuries. The weaker and poorer became his lord's sworn follower, or vassal, promising loyalty and service during his lifetime.

By the twelfth century every member of society owed service to someone higher up: peasant to baron, baron to count, count to duke, and finally duke to king, the only one without an overlord. Though the king, at the top of the pyramid, was supposed to be the real ruler, that was not always so. The man with the most vassals (the wealthy vassals—those who

A ninth-century church, built for safety on a rocky summit at the time of the Viking terror.

could afford horse and armor—were the powerful knights) and the most land was often more powerful than the king. Such was the case when Eleanor was born: her father, Duke William X of Aquitaine, owned more land, had more vassals, and was more powerful than the King of France, Louis VI, better known as Louis the Fat.

Troubadours play and sing to a lady, while nobles, in the background, ride off to the hunt. (From a medieval manuscript painting, as are most of the illustrations in this book.)

I

The Duchess
and the Prince

The French King, Louis the Fat, lay dying in his
hunting lodge where he had been taken to escape
the summer heat, the flies, and the stench of Paris.
His hands shook with palsy, and his bleary eyes
could hardly see. Recently he had grown so fat that
he could no longer mount a horse or bend over to
tie his shoes.

In spite of these physical handicaps and the fact
that he had not long to live, Louis' mind was as
sharp as ever. He deserved a better nickname, for
he had been a hardworking monarch, riding
throughout his royal domain, seeing that justice
was done, asserting his and his people's rights against
unruly barons. He had earned the respect and gained

the support of his subjects within his little kingdom, a small area surrounding the city of Paris. But the lands beyond his borders—today the rest of France— were a constant threat and worry to the King. Many of the huge states like Aquitaine were.bigger and richer than his own kingdom. Though the lords of these lands were his vassals and owed him allegiance, many had grown independent and dared defy him. Louis dreamed of a time when a French king would be the one and only ruler over all these lands, united into one nation. And Louis had one source of power that his vassals did not have—he had the backing of the church and the Pope, who had crowned and anointed him. He was King by divine right, and he owed allegiance to no man.

Louis worried nonetheless. His eldest son, trained to be the next king, had been killed in a riding accident, and his younger son had been snatched from a cathedral school to fill the role of prince. Trained to be a monk, the frail young Louis hardly seemed to fit the role of a future king. His early religious training was so deeply ingrained that he did not take easily to the necessary instruction in knighthood and statesmanship. The King wondered if his son would be able to cope with the rough world beyond his borders.

While Louis' great hulk tossed and sweated uncomfortably on his sickbed, messengers arrived with startling, urgent news: His wealthiest vassal, the Duke of Aquitaine, had suddenly died, leaving his vast estates to his teenage daughter, Eleanor. This seemed the very answer to Louis' prayer. As king he had the right to dispose of his vassal's daughter in marriage. If he could marry her to his son, the Prince, in one swift stroke he would attach the great Duchy of Aquitaine securely to the crown. The richest and fairest lands of western Europe would at last be under royal power.

There was no time to lose, for when news of the Duke's death leaked out—it was still a secret even in Aquitaine—it was likely that some bold and grasping knight would kidnap the young Duchess and bear her off to his high-walled castle and claim her land for himself. Louis immediately made arrangements for the Prince to gather a large body of knights and, with all speed, ride south to claim his prize.

The prize of Aquitaine was a lovely high-spirited girl of fifteen. Her long braids fell below her waist, and her deep-set eyes sparkled with mischief and gaiety. She knew how to please and was well aware of her beauty, charm, and wit. Scarcely had the news of her father's death come to her when messengers galloped into her courtyard to tell her that Prince Louis was on his way to claim her as a bride.

Prince Louis knew little about Duchess Eleanor herself except her fame for beauty and intelligence. It was her land, more than twice the size of the French kingdom, that interested the royal family. The fair land of Aquitaine stretched from the Loire River in the north to the borders of Spain, from the limestone heights of central France to the Atlantic

Ocean. Long ago the Romans had named it Aquatania, land of waters, for the many rivers that flowed through its rich, fertile valleys. Wild strawberries, raspberries, and dark-red cherries grew in abundance; fat sheep grazed in its lush green meadows. There were acres and acres of vineyards, olive groves, and wheat fields. High cliffs were natural sites for fortresses, and behind the hilltop castles stretched cool, dark forests. The Aquitanians were fiercely proud and independent, quick to anger and violent in battle. They were eager for adventure and passionate in love. They spent their days hunting or jousting in tournaments, their warm evenings dancing and singing in their castle courtyards. Much of their knowledge of music, song, and dance came from nearby Spain, where the Moors had long cultivated those arts in their highly civilized courts. The Aquitanians led a more elegant and carefree life than the serious, devout northerners, who thought the southerners frivolous, their women overdressed and madeup, their men show-offs with smooth, parted hair and shaved faces. The Aquitanians scorned the northerners as backward, narrow-minded, and uncouth. North and south were worlds apart.

Eleanor was a true Aquitanian, willful and independent. She had inherited her family's love of poetry and adventure. As a little girl she had listened with rapture to her grandfather, Duke William IX, singing romantic love songs. He was the first known troubadour—a poet-musician who composed his own verses and melodies and sang them for entertainment. In those days most people wrote in Latin, but Duke William used the common dialect everybody could understand and enjoy. William was also the very model of a courteous, gallant knight, an ideal Eleanor would never forget. She knew the exciting story of his elopement—how his lady love had escaped from her castle one night and galloped off with him, her arms clasped around his waist. This strong-willed grandmother did pretty much as she pleased, caring little what people thought or said about her. Eleanor had a good deal of her grandparents in her makeup.

Eleanor's father was a powerful, courageous knight, but he lacked her grandfather's charm and ability to compose and sing songs. Little is known about her mother—there were no exciting stories about her—who died when Eleanor was only eight years old. From then on Eleanor and her younger sister, Petronilla, had few restraints. But by the age of eight, Eleanor, like all the southern girls of noble birth, had already learned to sew, to weave and embroider, to play the harp, to sing and dance— many troubadour songs were composed to be danced as well as sung. She could ride a horse as well as any boy and often preferred riding astride to the more ladylike sidesaddle. Eleanor could also read and write, a rare accomplishment for a girl of the Middle Ages.

With her quick mind she went far in her studies, but it was on travels with her father, Duke William X, that she learned more useful things. Every year her father gathered his entire household, his family, his trusted knights and their squires, scribes, minstrels, chaplains, and servants, and set off to make the rounds of his estates. He checked up on his vassals, having them kneel before him to renew their oaths of loyalty. He collected the shares of eggs, vegetables, chickens, hogs, and barrels of wine due him from the peasants, sacks of flour from millers, and tolls at bridges. At the end of each day the Duke and his entire assemblage rode over the drawbridge to some vassal's castle, where they were welcomed for the night. Eleanor loved the evening entertainment. While they dined and drank the rich, red Aquitanian wine, minstrels chanted deeds of ancient heroes, acrobats turned themselves inside out, jugglers tossed shimmering knives high in the air and caught them without so much as a scratch, and troubadours sang their songs of love. Then, to the music of fiddles and the rhythmic beat of castanets, couples danced the fandango or groups, clapping and singing, danced the more rustic round dances. Eleanor danced far into the night. She had no mother to send her to bed.

Through these travels Eleanor began to understand her father's role as duke and what it took to rule a duchy. She met people from all walks of life—pilgrims in gray sackcloth, merchants from overseas, pathetic beggars, as well as highborn ladies, knights, and bishops. She knew far more about the world than her future husband, Prince Louis, who still preferred the quiet of the cloisters to the rough outside world, the companionship of monks and priests to that of knights and adventurers. Though Louis had docilely accepted his role as a future king, he had little confidence in himself. He was just sixteen, a year older than Eleanor, and he knew nothing about girls.

The King provided his son with an escort of five hundred knights to guide him through the dangerous and rebellious country south of the Loire River. Besides the mounted knights there were innumerable servants, who went on foot, and slow-moving mule-drawn carts, laden with tents, pavilions, and cooking utensils. At best the huge cavalcade probably made about fifteen miles a day. When they passed into Aquitaine, the heat became so intense that they traveled by night and rested by day. It took them almost a month to reach the outskirts of Bordeaux, where Eleanor was waiting.

Duchess Eleanor, now the richest heiress in western Europe, was as confident as Prince Louis was timid. She knew what she wanted and usually got it, but one thing even she did not question was the marriage arrangement. She had always known that she would be married off to some proud nobleman, more eager for her land than for herself. Things had always been that way. At least she was marrying a prince.

From a window in her castle tower, Eleanor could see the royal suite pitching their brightly colored tents and pavilions on the meadow across the river. There was no bridge, and the Prince had to be ferried over the water to meet his unknown bride.

Prince Louis was hardly the knightly warrior type that Eleanor was used to, but still, he was nicelooking, tall, with blond hair and mild blue eyes. For his part, Louis was enraptured with Eleanor's beauty, if a little shocked at her extravagant dress, her free-and-easy manner. Even more shocking to the innocent young Prince were the dancing and love songs he heard during the festivities before the wedding day.

Bells pealed out and trumpets blared as the wedding procession started through the cobbled streets of Bordeaux, passing housefronts gaily decorated with hanging tapestries and banners, to the old Romanesque church of St. Andrew. Tall tapers lighted the dark interior, incense filled the air, and the chants of choirboys resounded as Louis and Eleanor exchanged marriage vows. Immediately after the wedding they were crowned Duke and Duchess of Aquitaine.

Sitting beside Louis at the high table, Eleanor presided over the wedding feast with an ease and style beyond her fifteen years, seeing that all her guests had their fill of food and drink, calling on performers to entertain between courses, and graciously accepting her vassals' praises. The feast went on from midmorning to midafternoon as course after course was served by young pages. There were lobsters, oysters, mullet, and sole drowned in spicy

Musicians entertain while nobles dine.

sauces; roasts of pork and venison hot from the spit; platters of chicken, duck, cranes, and peacocks; vegetable pies and breads; all washed down with red and white wines. Last came a variety of fruits, figs, and all sorts of berries, served with little sweet tarts. Before the drowsy guests staggered to their feet, servants passed basins of water and towels for their greasy hands. Much of the meal was eaten with the fingers—forks had not yet come into common use—and leftover meat bones were tossed to the dogs lurking beneath the tables.

During this long feast and its between-courses entertainment, Eleanor could not help but notice how shy and uncomfortable Louis seemed. Perhaps he would change. His very meekness suggested to her that she might be able to mold him to her ideal of a man.

No sooner was the wedding celebration ended than the young couple and their escort headed north for Paris, stopping in Poitiers, the ancient walled capital of Poitou, Aquitaine's most important county. Since the dukes of Aquitaine were also counts of Poitou, Louis and Eleanor were crowned Count and Countess of Poitou in another elaborate ceremony. The ancestral castle in Poitiers was Eleanor's favorite home, and she and Louis stayed in the lovely tower built by her grandfather for his lady love. Here Eleanor opened the great oaken family treasure chest and generously bestowed gifts on her husband and guests. Generosity had been bred into Eleanor in her early childhood; along with hospitality, generosity was expected of every noble man and woman. Among her gifts to Louis was a delicate crystal-and-gold vase, inlaid with precious jewels. It can be seen today in Paris' Louvre Museum, Eleanor's only possession to survive.

Though Louis and the French guests were all exhausted and had had their fill of entertainment and ceremonies, Eleanor, full of her boundless energy, arranged another round of frenzied activity with hunting and hawking parties by day, feasting and dancing by night. But the merriment was abruptly interrupted one day when royal messengers galloped over the drawbridge to announce that King Louis the Fat had died. And so it was as King Louis VII and Queen Eleanor of France that the young couple approached the gates of Paris, the ancient capital of the French monarchs. But however much Eleanor looked forward to her queenly role, she was not prepared for Paris.

II

King and Queen

The heart of Paris was a little island in the Seine River known as the Ile de la Cité. To get to it, Eleanor and Louis had to pass through the noisy merchant suburb on the right bank of the river. They could see and hear the boatmen shouting as they unloaded barges full of fish, cattle, and salt, others groaning as they pushed barrels of wine and sacks of grain up the steep banks. Once they passed through the tower gate onto the fortified bridge, they had no view, for its thick, crenellated walls rose above their heads. A little beyond the bridge they entered the gateway to the royal castle, an ancient forbidding fortress built by early Franks long before. Louis led his bride up the long flight of worn steps into the great hall of the thick-walled tower. The only heat came from logs burning in an open hearth, filling the damp air with smoke. Through the narrow slits that served as windows, the river traffic could be heard but barely seen. Eleanor shivered in the dim, cold passage leading to a small bedroom, which appeared to be carved out of solid rock. Off one corner of this room was a little tower room, the latrine, with a round stone seat over a hole and long shaft leading down to a pit far below.

Outside the tower were the royal chapel, kitchens, stables, and a blacksmith's forge along the courtyard walls. The most appealing feature of this gloomy compound was the little garden, full of fruit trees and trellised vines, that ran down to the tip of the island, where the river's currents joined and flowed on their winding course northward to the sea.

Beyond the palace walls were noisy, crowded streets, darkened by overhanging upper stories of ancient wooden houses. Swine and goats roamed the dirty roads; vendors shouted out the prices of their wine and pastries. Each street proclaimed its own activity—the street of the Drapers, where cloth was sold; the Bakers' and Winesellers' streets; and the street of the Jews, where Jews loaned and changed money, mostly for students. One got used to the constant rumble of mill wheels and the loud pealing of church bells.

Eleanor found Paris dreary compared to her sunny south, the old castle primitive in contrast to the

Medieval shops in Paris.

ones she knew in Aquitaine with their tropical gardens, red-tiled courtyards, and fountains. She found the women prudish and dowdy—they had no sense of style—and the men deadly serious compared to her pleasure-seeking Aquitanians. She missed her native dialect with its rhythmic beat, its singsong lilt. Eleanor was homesick, but she soon found out that at least Paris had its own excitement. It was the most popular center of learning in western Europe and swarmed with noisy students who came from all over to study there. Every student liked to boast that he had studied in Paris. From her garden wall Eleanor could see the little bridge that led to the left bank of the river, where most of the students lived. Teachers lived on the bridge itself, in tall wooden houses clinging to the edge in higgledy-piggledy fashion. They held classes wherever they could—on stairways or in spaces between houses, where they lectured from benches. The bridge was a good place to draw a crowd, and the bigger the audience, the better the teachers liked it.

The Queen, of course, could not become involved in student life on the bridge, but on certain days the royal garden was opened up to teachers and students. Sitting in the shade of a fruit tree, Eleanor listened intently to heated debates and lectures on morals, good and evil, and the laws of the church—all subjects new to her. She was even more intent on the rare occasions when some radical student dared to question traditions of the church. On a less lofty plane she heard some amusing discussions in logic, such as whether a pig being led to market was led by the rope or the man, or what the color of a shield is if it is painted white on one side and black on the other. Eleanor carefully noted the clever methods used in debate and absorbed many ideas that would be useful to her later.

As winter approached, the old castle seemed colder and drearier than ever. Eleanor was not one to accept things she did not like, and she soon set about making her new home more livable according to her standards. She brought in colored tapestries to hang on the bleak walls. She had some of the narrow slits widened into windows, and ordered shutters for use in cold weather. She hired masons to build a new fireplace against the wall, with a chimney to collect the smoke. Knowing and loving music as she did, Eleanor found the choir of the royal chapel so badly trained that she dismissed the choirmaster and hired another. She also reorganized the management of servants, whom she found slovenly, and insisted that they wash their hands before serving meals. She ordered them to change the rushes strewn on the stone floors more often—what with the droppings of pet parrots and falcons and the hunting dogs, few of whom were housebroken, the castle often smelled like a zoo.

It is not surprising that Eleanor soon ran into trouble with her mother-in-law, the Dowager Queen, who immediately took a dislike to her daughter-in-law. The old Queen had lived happily for years in the ancestral castle, and now Eleanor, in a whirlwind of activity, was turning everything upside down. The Queen Mother could see no good in Eleanor—one of those frivolous southern belles—and disapproved of everything she did. She complained that her daughter-in-law was using up the royal treasury on lavish entertainment, unnecessary silk gowns, and fur-lined robes. She found Eleanor, who was not seen praying very often, a most unsuitable wife for her pious Louis. Worst of all was the huge retinue of southern friends—knights, troubadours, musicians, and elegant ladies whom Eleanor had brought with her. The old castle could scarcely contain them all, and the singing and dancing, the laughter and joking that began to echo through the once quiet halls, were shocking to the old lady. Added to this was the growing scandal of Eleanor's sister, Petronilla, who made no secret of her love affair with an older, married man. Much to Eleanor's relief her mother-in-law finally decided she could no longer stand living in the same castle. She packed up her belongings and moved to a country estate.

Eleanor had triumphed over her nagging mother-in-law, but she was disappointed that she could not transform her husband into her ideal of a gallant knight. Louis had gone back to his monastic studies, and spent long hours praying on his knees in church. At least he made no objection to Eleanor's spendthrift ways, and though ill at ease with her southern friends, he sometimes joined their festivities. Even if he disapproved of Eleanor's behavior, he adored her. He wanted her to be happy and he wanted her love. This may account for Louis' occasional rash and unpredictable actions. To prove to Eleanor that he was a strong king, he sometimes masked his timid nature and went to the other extreme. When the young couple got news of a revolt in Eleanor's favorite town of Poitiers, Louis reacted with surprising speed and ferocity. He would show his wife that he could handle her rebellious vassals! He and his knights sped to Poitiers so fast that they caught the rebels off-guard and quickly put down the rebellion, meting out unusually harsh punishments to all the townspeople. Then, as though he knew no other way to assert his kingly power, he brutally hacked off the hands of the rebel leaders.

Soon after this Louis got into double trouble, with both the church and his powerful vassal, the Count of Champagne, over the appointment of an archbishop. Louis stubbornly insisted on his choice of archbishop, while the Count backed an archbishop already appointed by the church. The Pope had to intervene and wrote Louis a letter, scolding him for acting like a foolish schoolboy and telling him to stop defying the church. This humiliated and infuriated the young King and made him more stubborn than ever, much to Eleanor's delight. Louis had given his oath to support his archbishop. Eleanor agreed that he should not break an oath—part of the knightly code of honor, no doubt as important to her as the laws of the church. But oath or not, the Pope could not tolerate Louis' defiance and finally resorted to the most dreaded punishment: excommunication. Excommunication closed the doors of the church to Louis, denying him all church services; if he died still under the ban, his soul would be damned forever. Eleanor knew that her father and grandfather had been excommunicated several times and had simply ignored the punishment, but Louis was nothing like them.

That the pious Louis should be excommunicated was almost more than he could bear and more than his subjects could understand. They thought it impossible that their most Christian king could suffer such a fate. Yet some demon now seemed to possess the young King. He and Eleanor blamed all their troubles on their difficult vassal, the Count of

Champagne. (Eleanor had her own grudge against the Count for his interference in her sister's love affair.) Egged on by Eleanor, who so longed to have her husband prove himself a fearless knight, Louis gathered an army and invaded the Count's lands. His army attacked the poorly defended town of Vitry and set fire to its thatched huts and wooden houses. The townspeople, 1300 of them, fled to the cathedral for safety. Then it too caught fire as flames spread to its timbered roof, which collapsed on the men, women, and children trapped inside. All were consumed in flames.

This was too much for Louis. Horrified and stricken with guilt, he fell ill. The roar and crackling of the fire at Vitry, the cries of the people, haunted him constantly. He knew he deserved the wrath of God, and he feared for his very soul. He fasted and prayed continually. The Pope was impressed with Louis' sincere remorse and finally pardoned him. Still Louis remained depressed and ill. Even Eleanor could not raise his spirits.

Then Eleanor's spirits began to sink, but for a different reason. She had been married for some years now and had as yet produced no child. She longed for a baby, and she knew that all France expected her to provide a male heir to the throne. Could *she* have offended God too?

One person who might have prevented the young couple's rashness and steered them on a saner course was Louis' advisor, Abbot Suger, a tiny man of enormous energy and wisdom. But Suger had sensed that Eleanor and Louis had no desire for his or anyone's advice. He could see that Louis was so infatuated with his beautiful if headstrong wife that he would listen only to her. So Suger had tactfully left them alone and had immersed himself in a project of which he had dreamed for years—the rebuilding and beautification of the abbey church of St. Denis, the burial place for all French kings. Suger was transforming it with the most modern, radical architecture and filling it with beautiful works of art. It was a bold experiment such as no one had ever seen before. Now that it was almost finished, he came to Paris and turned his attention to the unhappy King.

Abbot Suger felt that Louis, still sick with remorse, had suffered enough. He now needed to be cheered up and to regain confidence so that he could rule his kingdom. Suger invited the King and Queen to the dedication of his abbey church and arranged that Louis have an important part in the religious ceremony.

Eleanor's spirits rose at once at the prospect of a diversion and a chance to put on her best finery. She and Suger had one thing in common—they both loved beautiful things. For the occasion Eleanor wore a gown of pure silk with tight-fitting sleeves, designed to show off her delicate wrists—as important as a slim ankle is today. Around her waist she wore a jeweled belt. Over her gown fell a long red velvet robe trimmed with fur; its full sleeves with their wide openings tapered to points that almost touched the ground. Over her hair was a scarf, called a wimple, held in place by her gold crown. Married women were supposed to cover their hair, considered by the church to be a snare for the Devil. But, like any woman's hat, a wimple could be attractive. Surely Eleanor arranged hers with an artistic flair. Her wrists were laden with bracelets, and long pendants hung from her ears. She looked every inch a queen; but Louis, dressed in a drab gray cloak, looked like a penitent monk. No one would have thought this was the man who had recently ravaged the countryside with fire and sword.

The royal procession moved slowly on its seven-mile journey from Paris to the walled abbey of St. Denis. The road was jammed with white-robed bishops, hooded monks and pilgrims, knights and ladies, and a motley group of curious peasants and beggars, all eager to see Suger's newfangled church.

The King, carrying a silver casket containing the sacred relics of the saint, led the procession through the wide new portals, heading for the high altar. A dazzling twenty-foot-high cross, glittering with precious gems and a gold figure of the crucified Christ, whose wounds were made of blood red rubies, first caught the people's gaze. But even more awe-inspiring was the chancel, with its soaring vaults and delicate chapels radiating like petals of a flower. The whole sanctuary was ablaze with light and color. Beautiful tall windows, with tiny bits of jewellike glass sparkling in a rainbow of colors, told stories of the Bible.

Suger and his masons had been trying to find a way to let more light into the dim old church. By

A late-nineteenth-century engraving of the "walls of glass" in a Gothic cathedral.

using intersecting arches and rib vaulting, the old-fashioned massive stone walls were no longer necessary to support the roof; in their place were what appeared to be walls of glass. And, as Suger had planned, the light, filtered through the stained-glass windows, appeared to come from Heaven itself.

Inspired by Suger's deep religious feeling, St. Denis was the first true example of what was later called Gothic architecture. It launched the period of great cathedral building in ever higher and more daring experiments.

Everyone was pleased with Suger's church and the uplifting service except one dignitary, Abbot Bernard, who disapproved and found all the gold and glitter distracting. He preferred simple, unadorned churches, where one's eyes should be closed in prayer and not be tempted to gaze at beautiful windows or precious works of art. Abbot Bernard, a mystic and a future saint, was famous for his miracle cures. Many considered him the holiest man in all Christendom. Tall and lean, he led a blameless life and was as strict with himself as he was with others. His fiery sermons on sin reduced the wicked to fear and trembling. If anyone could make a man repent, it was Abbot Bernard. As for women, he thought most of them—especially beautiful, alluring women like Eleanor—evil corruptors of men.

After the ceremony Bernard had a talk with the Queen. Most people lowered their eyes when talking to this holy man, but not Eleanor—she looked directly at him and answered him with ease, showing that she knew as much about royal and church affairs as any man. Her boldness quite shocked the Abbot. He also disapproved of Eleanor's elegant clothes, her perfume, and her eye shadow; the clinking of her bracelets and the bobbing of her earrings disturbed him. Suddenly he realized that she must be the evil demon who had bewitched and led the King astray. He urged her to be a better, more obedient wife and to stop meddling in the affairs of church and state.

Eleanor had wanted to talk to the Abbot, but she had not wanted a lecture. She wanted to beg a favor of him—that he use his holy influence and add his prayers to hers that she become a mother. The Abbot softened at this humble request. Perhaps his talk had done her some good.

Within a year Eleanor, now twenty-two, had her first child. It was not the longed-for male heir that Louis and the kingdom wanted, but a daughter whom they named Marie in honor of the Virgin Mary. Absorbed in the joys of being a mother, Eleanor stopped meddling in affairs of state for a while.

III

Crusade

Louis had made his peace with the church and with his vassal the Count of Champagne, but he felt he must do more to wash away his recent sins. Eleanor was discouraged to find him wearing a hair shirt and constantly praying again. He was thinking of going on a pilgrimage to the Holy Land to do penance at Christ's tomb when an even better opportunity arose. Word came to France that the infidel Moslem Turks had captured the Christian state of Edessa. Jerusalem itself would soon be in danger. Here was the perfect chance to purify his soul: to lead a crusade against the enemies of Christ.

There had already been one crusade, fifty years earlier, to rescue the Holy Land from the warlike

Turks who had captured it from the Arab Moslems. The Turks were Moslems themselves, but unlike the Arabs, who had occupied the Holy Land for centuries and treated Christians with respect, the Turks maltreated and barred Christian pilgrims from their sacred shrines in Jerusalem. Christians of the West were aroused to act, and the Pope himself took up the battle cry. Urging knights to stop their petty wars and to unite in a holy cause against the enemies of Christ, he launched the first and most successful of a long series of crusades against the Moslems. The crusaders captured Jerusalem and turned it into a Christian kingdom. Beguiled by the splendors of the Near East, many crusaders lingered on and set up little feudal principalities of their own.

Eleanor's grandfather had been on the first crusade, and even now her uncle, Count Raymond, was Prince of Antioch, to the north of Jerusalem. Raymond was only nine years older than Eleanor, and she remembered playing with him when she was a child. Raymond was in a dangerous position: Edessa, which had just fallen to the Turks, bordered his lands. If Antioch fell too, the enemy could easily sweep onward to Jerusalem. He sent the King and Queen his own, urgent request for help.

No one favored a crusade more than Louis, and he was overjoyed when the Pope chose him to lead it. Eleanor was just as eager for a crusade, but as usual, her reasons were not the same as Louis'. Though she, too, was touched by the religious fervor for a holy war, she mostly longed for adventure and to get away from Paris, where she found life with her meek, pious husband growing more and more boring. Even little Marie, now largely in the hands of nurses, failed to dispel the dreary monotony of Eleanor's life.

King Louis called an assembly to the little hill town of Vézelay. News that Abbot Bernard would speak brought such crowds that the church could not hold them all. On a platform set up on the hillside, the thin, frail Abbot addressed the multitude in his thunderous voice, urging all to forget their petty quarrels and to unite in this holy war. He promised forgiveness of sins and everlasting reward in heaven to those who "took the cross." A red cross on his tunic would be the crusader's sign.

"Crosses, crosses, give us crosses," shouted the people. King Louis was the first to take the cross, and overcome with emotion, he burst into tears and prostrated himself before the Abbot. Eleanor, too, took the cross and knelt before the holy man, offering her vassal knights from Aquitaine for the cause. Then others—barons, knights, churchmen, ladies, and humbler folk pressed forward to get their crosses. Bernard's supply soon gave out, so he flung off his cloak and snipped it into little crosses as more and more people pledged themselves for the crusade. The sun began to sink behind the hill, but still the people came. The cries of "God wills it" echoed down the misty valley.

Later a story spread that Eleanor and her lady

friends had slipped away after getting their crosses and returned riding on white horses, like ancient Amazons. Dressed in crusader tunics, high gilt boots, and plumed helmets, they dashed around the hillside, brandishing their swords and whipping up enthusiasm for the cause. There is no proof of this tale, but it is the kind of story that Eleanor's unconventional behavior often inspired.

One person who did not share the wild enthusiasm for this crusade was Abbot Suger. He worried that the King was not up to such leadership, that Louis' unstable and indecisive character might cause some new disaster, and he saw no reason for Eleanor, or any woman, to go crusading. He tried to dissuade the King and Queen, but they were both deeply committed and determined to go. Suger finally agreed to rule the kingdom in their absence.

While Louis prepared for the crusade by pious works, distributing alms to the poor and visiting monasteries, Eleanor went home to Aquitaine to gather her own vassal knights. Due to her efforts Aquitaine supplied more crusaders than any other one area. Then Eleanor went to work to raise money for the war—putting on tournaments for which she charged entrance fees, gathering proceeds from town fairs and granting privileges to monasteries in exchange for gold. She also gathered more lady friends, minstrels, and troubadours, all unfit for a holy war and expressly banned by Abbot Bernard. She didn't have to worry about the Abbot at the moment, for he had been sent to Germany to rally the reluctant Germans to join the crusade.

It took the French a whole year to gather an army and the supplies of arms, armor, horses, wagonloads of siege engines—catapults, battering rams, and movable towers—food, tents, and pavilions needed for this vast undertaking. Men were heard to grumble at the sight of so many chests of bedding, utensils, washbasins, silk dresses and fur-lined robes, trinkets, and cosmetics that Eleanor and her noble ladies insisted on bringing. They were going to look their best no matter what, but it was not at all clear just what purpose all these ladies with their maids were going to serve against the enemy. They looked more prepared for some grand tour of foreign cities than for a crusade. Certainly Eleanor looked forward to seeing more of the world, exotic places like Constantinople, Antioch, where her uncle Raymond lived in oriental splendor, and the white-walled holy city of Jerusalem. Eleanor expected a glorious adventure.

There was no grumbling, only wild excitement, when the great host assembled at Suger's abbey of St. Denis in June 1147. The Pope himself had come there to give his blessings to all crusaders. There were knights from Burgundy and Normandy, Eleanor's vassal knights from Aquitaine, Louis' from Paris and Champagne, foot soldiers from every village and farm. There were noble ladies with their maids-in-waiting and their troubadours; there were bishops, chaplains, and barefoot pilgrims, and following in the rear a rabble of undesirable hangers-on, beggars, and criminals hoping for salvation. With banners flying and the red crosses gleaming in the sun, the enormous cavalcade, the mightiest army of knights ever assembled by the French, started on its long journey to the East. The heavy tread of marching feet and the clatter of horses' hooves brought forth villagers to wave and cheer them on. People thrilled to see the Queen on horseback, her gorgeous robes covered with the white lilies of France, her saddle encrusted with silver. "Pray for us, Lady, in Jerusalem," they shouted.

Eleanor rode up front with her Aquitanian knights and friends and their imposing baggage train. The farther they got from Paris, the happier Eleanor became. She soon forgot her past boredom and the gloomy old palace on the Seine as new sights unfolded day by day. At times she even forgot her husband, who had chosen to bring up the rear of the army and was a long way off, in back of the endless rows of knights, foot soldiers, and wagons of war equipment. Though Eleanor was now twenty-five, she felt like a young girl again among her old friends. Soon the sound of flute and fiddle was heard as minstrels played and sang. Other pleasures had not been forgotten—Eleanor and the ladies had brought along their pet falcons (also forbidden by Abbot Bernard), tied to their wrists. When wild ducks or cranes were spotted circling overhead, the ladies removed the hoods covering their falcons' heads and released them to chase the wild birds. At the blowing of a small silver whistle, the well-trained falcons brought back the prey to their owners. The warm summer days and soft moonlit nights passed quickly in the beginning of this great adventure.

Traveling ten to twenty miles a day through Germany and across the plains of Hungary, the army took three months to get to Constantinople. The glamor of the crusade had begun to wear a little thin by the time the army approached this great walled city, the richest and biggest city of eastern Europe, capital of the Byzantine Empire, and gateway to the Near East. Food had begun to give out, and soldiers took to pillaging farms and villages though under strict orders not to. Louis was incapable of disciplining his troops, who were greeted with less and less enthusiasm, sometimes even with hostility, when they drew near towns. Then Louis learned disturbing news: The Germans who were to join him at Constantinople had not waited and had already crossed to Asia.

The King and Queen and other nobles were invited into Constantinople while the bulk of the army camped outside its walls. What a city! Eleanor was overwhelmed by its dazzling beauty, its white marbles, its gold and bronze statues, its bright mosaics. She and the King were lodged in one of the emperor's palaces overlooking the harbor, where the golden domes of churches reflected in the clear, blue waters below. Eleanor walked between shaded colonnades, looking at the many shops full of oriental silks and precious jewels, or on tiled paths through beautiful gardens where cooling fountains played. In the palace she walked on soft Persian carpets and bathed in marble tubs. What a contrast to the dirty, rush-covered floors and wooden tubs in Paris! Like an eager tourist, Eleanor drank in all she

King Louis (on black horse) and crusaders arrive at the walls of Constantinople. (The artist painted in the German King [on white horse], though in fact he had already gone on to the Near East.)

could in their two weeks' stay, visiting churches where impeccably trained choirs sang to perfection, the hippodrome where chariots raced, and the harbor where ships from every nation were moored. She was enchanted and impressed by the elegance and refinement of court life and noticed, to her dismay, how boorish the crusaders seemed compared to the emperor and his courtiers. Louis, in his simple garb, appeared an awkward schoolboy next to the cultivated Emperor Manuel, dressed in exquisitely embroidered robes and sitting on a golden throne. People did not just kneel before him—they prostrated themselves at his feet.

What surprised Eleanor was the Empress Bertha, a dumpy German with no sense of style and so different from her suave, sophisticated husband. Bertha belonged to the German imperial family, and Eleanor couldn't help thinking how political marriages, like this one and her own, united such unsuitable husbands and wives. Oh, why could she not have had the good fortune to marry a man like Manuel! She could have filled the role of empress so well.

Though Eleanor and Louis could sense that the Emperor was not too friendly—indeed, he was afraid of what the horde of crude crusaders might do to his beautiful city—they were lavishly entertained. Served by well-disciplined slaves, they feasted on rare delicacies and wines, cooled in snow from the mountains. They listened to strange harmonies of eastern music and watched sinuous dancers and acrobats while nearby fountains jetted perfumed water.

Unlike Eleanor, Louis found all the ceremony and luxury exaggerated and even distasteful. He didn't quite trust Emperor Manuel, and had heard that he had made some kind of a deal with the enemy Turks. He was impatient to be off, to catch up with the Germans. He almost had to drag his wife away. By this time Eleanor was as disenchanted with her husband as she was enchanted with Constantinople.

Once in Asia, hardships and horrors confronted the crusaders daily. They learned that more than half the German crusading army had been annihilated by the Turks, and came upon their corpses rotting by the roadside. Eleanor and the ladies shuddered at the sight—they were not prepared for this ordeal. Soon they met survivors heading back, ready to abandon the whole crusade and return home. Louis finally persuaded the German leader to join forces and, after much changing of his mind, decided to take the longer and more circuitous route along the shore, thinking it safer from enemy attack than the more direct inland route.

But it was not safe from early-winter storms and flash floods. After a terrible Christmas Day, when the raging torrent of a flooding river swept men, horses, and equipment out to sea, Louis changed his mind again. Way behind schedule, he decided to try the shorter, inland route. This meant crossing lofty, desolate mountains in winter weather. Eleanor wondered if Louis knew what he was doing.

It was difficult indeed to get the heavily armed knights, the huge baggage train of equipment, and the ladies' wagon loads up the narrow, winding mountain paths. The women, well protected in the center of the cavalcade, were carried in litters slung between two horses when jogging on horseback became too hard. They still slept in comfort, on beds in tents or pavilions set up every night, but the music and singing had ceased.

Surprise enemy attacks began to harass the

Christian army. The crusader knights were used to charging head-on against an enemy in the open, but the Turks used guerilla tactics. They would suddenly appear as if from nowhere astride their swift ponies, let loose a volley of arrows, and then vanish.

Louis changed his commanders as often as he changed his mind. One day he put one of Eleanor's Aquitanian vassals in charge of the vanguard, with orders that it proceed to the summit of the lofty Mount Cadmos, which loomed ahead, to set up camp on the flatland there and wait for the others to catch up. Louis, in charge of the rear guard, lagged far behind the long line of slow-moving baggage carts, pilgrims, and foot soldiers. He misjudged time and distance, and the vanguard, with the ladies and the bulk of mounted knights but no baggage, easily reached the summit in the early afternoon. From the cold, windblown top could be seen a more protected and inviting place to spend the night. With no enemy in sight, it seemed silly to wait—the others would find them. Disobeying the King's orders, the Aquitanian commander decided to move on down the other side of the mountain to the better campsite. Thus the vanguard lost contact with, and was out of sight of, the rest of the army.

Meanwhile Louis and the rear guard moved slowly and laboriously up the steep incline. Knights took off their armor to ease the climb, horses and men strained to get the wagons up the torturous path. The Turks, who had been watching all these movements from their hideouts, suddenly burst forth from under cover on their small, swift horses. Shouting, "Allah is our God," they let fly their arrows. Then, brandishing their curved swords right and left, they slashed at their unarmed enemy. Boulders loosened; men, horses, and wagons hurtled over the precipices to the gorges below. Quickly arming, Louis and his bodyguard joined the battle, trying to fend off the enemy as best they could. But one by one his knights were killed, some losing their grip and sliding over the edge of the narrow pass, some felled by the Turks. Louis in his chain mail and crusader tunic looked no different from other knights and luckily was not recognized as the King, a prize the Turks would not have let slip out of their hands. Almost alone, he grabbed hold of some tree roots and swung himself up onto a boulder. With his back to the mountain, he fought off his assailants until darkness fell and the enemy melted away. Not until midnight did scouts sent by the vanguard find the dazed and wounded King and the other survivors.

After this, French dislike for the Aquitanians, whose leader had disobeyed the King's orders, mounted daily. Soon the French were fabricating stories in which they blamed Eleanor, too, for the disaster at Mount Cadmos. But the real trouble was Louis' poor judgment and lack of military know-how. It became clearer every day that he was not the man to lead a crusade.

There were still more mountains to cross, winter storms with howling winds and blinding rains, and always enemy attacks to cope with. Eleanor and the women had their share of horrors and discomfort when tents blew over and downpours soaked their bedding and clothes. Food and water gave out at times, and the army was reduced to eating horsemeat and drinking animal blood. Some crusaders gave up their arms and armor in exchange for food. The glorious adventure had become a nightmare. It was a famished, tattered army that finally reached the coast, where they decided to make the rest of the journey to the Holy Land by sea. Unfortunately not enough ships could be hired to take them all, so those who could afford it—the King and Queen, the nobles, knights, and bishops—set off, leaving the foot soldiers and pilgrims to go on over more mountains through enemy territory as best they could. Of those left behind, many died of sickness or starvation; others became Moslems in exchange for bread and disappeared from history. Only a handful made it to the Holy Land.

After three weeks of stormy passage the King and Queen, worn and seasick, arrived at the port near Antioch. Suddenly it was spring—the hillsides green, flowers blooming everywhere. Eleanor's uncle Raymond, Prince of Antioch, was there to greet them, their warmest welcome during the whole crusade. The nightmare of those mountain passes and storms, the starvation and enemy attacks, quickly faded from Eleanor's mind. The ancient city of Antioch reminded Eleanor of her hometown of Bordeaux, with its tropical plants and its river full of ships. Antioch was at the crossroads of traffic for spices

and silks from the Orient, ivory and grain from
Egypt, cedars from Lebanon. Some of the ships, she
knew, would make their way across the Mediterranean Sea and come to rest in the river below her
castle in Bordeaux. Eleanor gazed with wonder and
delight at Antioch's steeply terraced gardens rising
on its hills, at its ancient Greek and Roman temples
intermingling with Christian churches and Moslem
minarets. To her surprise she noticed turbaned
Moslem merchants talking freely to Christians from
the West. Perhaps not all Moslems were enemies of
Christ. Eleanor found Antioch less grand than Constantinople, but more interesting and more friendly.

The friendliness was mostly due to Eleanor's uncle
Raymond, who did everything he could to entertain
the crusaders and make them feel at home. Like
Eleanor's grandfather, Raymond was Eleanor's ideal
of a perfect knight, handsome and powerfully built,
brave in battle yet courteous and gentle with the
ladies. With the generosity that Eleanor expected
of a true knight, Raymond provided a variety of
entertainment—hunting and hawking for the men,
feasts of spicy eastern food, music and dancing for
all. He showered attention on Eleanor and gave her
costly gifts of oriental silks, jewels, and perfumes.
In his company Eleanor's youth and vitality revived. She soon felt completely relaxed and at home.
It was such a relief to talk in her own dialect with
someone she had known so well as a child, with
someone she felt understood her. She confided to
her sympathetic uncle her unhappiness as a queen

married to such a dull, monkish husband, and how homesick she had been in Paris. Raymond, impressed by Eleanor's intelligence, confided in her his military plans and was pleased to find she understood their merits. They talked of many things and recalled their childhood adventures in Aquitaine. Louis noticed with pain their intimate laughing and joking, much of which he could not understand. He thought his wife had never looked happier or more beautiful. He thought—or rather imagined—that she was flirting with her uncle. Louis was annoyed. Louis was jealous.

Though Raymond enjoyed talking to Eleanor and her Aquitanians, his friendliness to Louis and other crusaders had political motives as well. After all, they had come partly at his request to rescue the Holy Land from the enemy, and he had been waiting for their arrival for months. He wanted to use Louis' army to help his own small forces attack the neighboring areas, in the hands of the Moslem Turks, before they attacked him and opened the way for themselves to Jerusalem. It was the most sensible plan, Eleanor agreed. Louis objected and insisted that he would make no war until he had visited Jerusalem and fulfilled his vows to do penance for his sins. Arguments went on for days. Louis grew more adamant, Raymond more angry, and Eleanor more and more annoyed with her husband, who seemed to think saving his soul more important than saving the Holy Land.

Finally things came to a head. Louis told Eleanor

to pack up, that they were leaving for Jerusalem the next day. Eleanor flew into a rage: Louis could go on alone—under no circumstances would she leave Antioch. She would stay with her own vassals to help carry out her uncle's military plans. The quarrel grew more heated and more personal. Louis reminded Eleanor that she was his vassal and wife, that she must obey him. At this Eleanor blurted out what may have been on her mind for a long time— that she wanted a divorce! She would willingly give up her queen's crown to be an independent woman. Louis was stunned, but Eleanor was eager to argue her point, and she knew her church law well. She now delivered a savage blow. She told Louis that she was not really his wife, that they were fourth cousins, too closely related in the eyes of the church to be lawfully married. In fact, she said, they were living in sin; she reminded Louis that no less a person than the awesome Abbot Bernard had said so. The stricken King began to brood. He remembered that Abbot Bernard had opposed their marriage but that the Pope had been willing to ignore the kinship. Perhaps their marriage was cursed, for Eleanor had produced only one daughter and no male heir.

With Eleanor's words ringing in his ears, Louis straightway sought his chaplains for advice. They too fell into a panic. What would happen to the crusade without Eleanor's vassals? What would become of the Kingdom of France without Eleanor's wealthy land of Aquitaine? And what of the scandal and the King's reputation? They advised Louis to waste no time—to abduct the Queen and bear her off secretly to Jerusalem.

For once Louis acted quickly and decisively. Before dawn the crusader army marched out of the gates of Antioch without so much as a good-by to their host and headed toward Jerusalem. Concealed somewhere was the Queen, a prisoner under guard. Such treatment hardly helped patch the quarrel between the royal couple. And Eleanor was not so well guarded that the rank and file didn't soon learn about their Queen's arrest. What terrible thing had she done to deserve this? Stories arose and scandalmongers painted lurid pictures of Eleanor's misconduct in Antioch, suggesting that she had had an affair with her uncle Raymond. Those ten short days in that beautiful city would hound her the rest of her life.

Within the Holy City of Jerusalem Louis at last did penance for his sins at the tomb of Christ. This was the only consolation of the whole Crusade, which now began to fall apart. Having refused Raymond's wise advice in Antioch, Louis now listened to foolish advice—to attack the enemy in the strong-walled city of Damascus. After a four-day siege the crusaders got nowhere. Quarrels broke out among the leaders, who kept changing methods and places of attack. When they heard that large numbers of Moslem reinforcements were on their way to help Damascus, the crusaders retreated in wild confusion, pursued by the enemy.

Nothing had been accomplished to further the Christian cause in the Holy Land, only great loss of life and equipment. Abbot Bernard cried out in anguish at the news, "The Lord, provoked by our sins, has judged the world with justice but not with His usual mercy." Abbot Suger was not so surprised at the disaster. He knew that Louis was a very Christian king but somewhat simpleminded when it came to military affairs.

Two years after the crusaders had set out with such high hopes and ambitions, such promise of success, the sad and humiliated King set sail for home, having lost a war and perhaps a wife. Eleanor followed in a separate ship, a two-masted, high-pooped vessel. There was little comfort aboard and always considerable danger in crossing the Mediterranean Sea, where sudden storms played havoc with·the unwieldly pilgrim ships and pirates were on the lookout for treasure. The little fleet had just rounded the tip of Greece when they found themselves heading into a naval battle between the Greeks and Sicilians. Suddenly the Greeks bore down upon the crusader ships, pirated the Queen's vessel with its valuable hostage, and sped off to the north. Sicilian war galleys went in hot pursuit and rescued the Queen within a few days. No sooner had the fleet reassembled and set its sails for France than a great storm arose. Wild winds blew down from the north, huge waves rocked and battered the ships, which soon lost sight of each other. For more than a month no word was heard from either King or

Wild winds and huge waves batter the crusader ships.

Queen. They had been given up for dead by the time Louis finally landed at the foot of Italy, vowing never to board a ship again and sick with anxiety about the fate of his Queen. A few weeks later he learned that Eleanor, whose ship had been driven as far as North Africa, had landed in Sicily. The royal couple were reunited, but Eleanor, exhausted and weak from her rough sea voyage, took little comfort in the reunion. She had news at this time that only increased her bitterness toward Louis. Her uncle Raymond had been killed in battle against superior forces of the Turks. So elated were the Turks at the death of their formidable foe that they sent his severed head in a silver casket to the Caliph of Baghdad. Louis' refusal to heed Raymond's advice had contributed to the failure of the crusade and now, Eleanor felt sure, to her uncle's death.

Abbot Suger, who had heard of Louis and Elea-

nor's quarrel, had arranged for the unhappy couple
to have an audience with the Pope on their way
back to Paris. Eleanor hoped to persuade the Pope
to grant a divorce and had her arguments ready.
But the Pope was moved to pity by Louis who, despite the quarrel, so obviously still loved his wife.
With all the skill of a marriage counselor, the Pope
tried to heal the breach between the couple. He
assured them that his blessing had made their marriage lawful. Louis was delighted, Eleanor in despair. For the moment, however, it seemed that the
marriage was mended.

IV

Eleanor and the Duke

Things were not as well as they seemed. Not for Eleanor. The Pope had let her down and she felt trapped. Was she to be tied forever to her dull, simpleminded husband, whom she could neither admire nor love?

Paris did nothing to raise Eleanor's spirits. She and Louis returned to an unusually cold, severe winter. The little island on the Seine seemed frozen in silence, the rumble of mill wheels stilled by the river's ice, the streets empty of noisy students, who huddled indoors wherever they could find a warm hearth.

Even though Abbot Suger had done his best to make the old castle warm and cheerful, it could hardly compare with those white marble palaces bathed in sunshine and glittering with mosaics in the exotic cities of the Near East. The excitement and adventures of the crusade were only a memory now, and life around her more boring and gloomy than ever.

Worse than the winter's frost were the icy glances of the French, who had always disapproved of her. Those eager to slander Eleanor revived and spread the malicious gossip about her conduct in Antioch. It was whispered—not too softly—that the Queen was an adulteress. And, forgetting Louis' ineptitude, some even blamed her for the failure of the whole crusade.

Added to this humiliation was the fact that Eleanor no longer shared the government with Louis. Persuaded by his clergymen not to trust her, he no longer sought her advice as he had in their early married years. Yet Eleanor was wiser and better equipped than ever to exert her power as a queen. She seethed inwardly, feeling her youth slipping away in dull monotony as Louis became more pious and morose every day. Everywhere she looked she saw priests padding through the halls, everywhere she listened she heard the mumbling of prayers. The castle seemed more like a monastery than a royal castle. No more music, no more songs, no more dancing, no more adventures. In despair she cried out, "I thought I married a king, but I find I have married a monk."

Even the fact that Eleanor was going to have a

baby did little to cheer her up. Should it be the longed-for male heir, she knew all would be forgiven but that her fate would be sealed. She would remain a captive queen forever.

In the spring Eleanor gave birth to another daughter, whom they named Alix. She had failed again as a queen—a queen who could not produce a son was worse than useless. Yet her very failure gave Eleanor new hope. Now, at last, she might persuade Louis that their marriage was cursed. With only two daughters in fourteen years of marriage, surely she could convince him to divorce her. Eleanor's spirits rose at once, but she knew she would have to be patient.

As long as Abbot Suger was alive, he managed to keep the couple together. Always thinking of the good of the realm, he pointed out to Eleanor and Louis that they were still young and that they would have a son someday. He warned Louis that a divorce would bring disaster on the kingdom, losing, as it would, Eleanor's great Duchy of Aquitaine, its greatest source of wealth and power. Even now there was a new threat to the kingdom—the rising power of young Duke Henry of Normandy. Without Aquitaine what would happen to the little kingdom of France?

But the wise little Abbot was almost eighty, and in the winter following Alix's birth he died. Without his voice of reason, Louis gave up his struggle against Eleanor's desire for separation, and she was able to press for a divorce. Also, Louis had begun to fear that his beautiful wife might never have a son, that his dynasty might come to an end.

Before Louis could make up his mind about divorce, he had a matter to settle with two of his difficult vassals, Geoffrey the Fair, Count of Anjou, and his son Henry of Normandy. Geoffrey the Fair, one of the handsomest and most courteous knights in Europe, was more often called by his nickname, Plantagenet, because of his habit of wearing a sprig of broom plant—*planta genista*—in his cap. His son Henry, if not as handsome, was equally dashing and charming. It was known that both father and son had violent tempers. There was a current saying about the family: "From the devil they came, to the devil they will go." Like Eleanor's family, they did pretty much as they pleased.

In the summer following Suger's death, King Louis summoned Geoffrey and Henry to Paris—Geoffrey to answer a charge of treason for having captured a king's high officer and imprisoned him in a thick walled dungeon. Geoffrey and the officer were old enemies, and had been battling for three years over a strip of land bordering their counties. Geoffrey had taken a whole year to batter down his enemy's castle and capture him. He was not about to give up his prisoner, his own fair prize of battle, whether he was a king's officer or not. That Abbot Bernard had excommunicated Geoffrey for this crime against the crown didn't bother him a bit. Henry had been summoned to pay his long overdue homage to the King in order to be recognized Duke of Normandy.

Louis feared and distrusted the ambitious young Henry. It was high time he came to give his oath of allegiance to his king.

It was a hot, stifling day—the kind to make tempers short—when Geoffrey and his son arrived at the royal castle. Eleanor, Louis, and Abbot Bernard, who would act as mediator, along with other great barons of the realm, were waiting in the castle hall. No one was quite prepared for the sight that greeted them as father and son strode into the hall. Geoffrey was dragging behind him the King's officer, ignominiously bound in chains like some common criminal. The sight of the royal prisoner caused a stir among the dignitaries. When Abbot Bernard reminded Geoffrey that it was a crime and a sin to hold the King's officer and demanded his release, Geoffrey flew into a rage. He angrily and flatly refused. Almost shouting at the Abbot, he added that if it was a sin in God's eyes, then he would go on living in sin. Shocked at this blasphemy, Abbot Bernard rose up, his eyes blazing with heavenly wrath. In his thunderous voice he predicted that Geoffrey would come to an untimely death. This dire prophecy did not have the desired effect. Angered but not intimidated, Geoffrey turned his back on the Abbot and stalked out of the hall, dragging his prisoner and followed by his son.

Eleanor had been watching this interview with interest. Though amused at Geoffrey's behavior, she was mostly interested in his son Henry, whom she had never seen before. During the interview he never sat down but paced restlessly to and fro, as though impatient to get the business over with. Eleanor couldn't keep her eyes off him. She noticed every detail—his bold gray eyes, his ruddy, freckled cheeks, his bright-red hair, his rough hands, and his legs, somewhat bowed by life in the saddle. She approved his broad shoulders, his fine athletic body, full of energy and ready to spring into action at a moment's notice. She could tell that he didn't care what others thought of his looks, wearing, as he did, an unstylishly short cape flung carelessly over his shoulders. There was nothing timid or monkish about young Henry, and Eleanor found him irresistible.

A few days after this stormy interview something very strange happened: Geoffrey and Henry returned to the castle in a completely different mood. Full of smiles and courtesy, they not only offered to release the royal prisoner but volunteered to give King Louis a small but important bit of borderland as a gesture of goodwill and desire for peace. This bit of land, called the Vexin, lay between France and Normandy, and had been long fought over by the French and Normans. Then young Henry stepped forth to pay homage to King Louis. Kneeling, he placed his hands in Louis' palms, promising to be a faithful vassal and to defend the King against his enemies. Louis then gave Henry the kiss of peace and pronounced him Duke of Normandy.

The French, though pleased, were baffled at this complete turnaround. Some thought it no less than

A young knight kneels in homage to his overlord.

one of Abbot Bernard's miracles. Others wondered
if the Queen had had anything to do with it. Had

there been some secret bargain behind closed doors? That Geoffrey and Henry had so willingly given up the Vexin seemed to suggest a greater prize within their grasp. There was much gossip but no good answer. In fact, among the French only Eleanor knew the answer, and she kept it a deep secret.

Count Geoffrey and Duke Henry left for home in high spirits, with Paris none the wiser. As they neared their castle in Anjou, the weather became unbearably hot and they paused to take a cooling swim in a stream. The sudden cold had disastrous results for Geoffrey, who came down with chills and a fever. Within three days he lay dead, fulfilling, so it seemed, Bernard's dire prophecy.

Even before the news of Geoffrey's death reached Paris, the city was buzzing with new gossip—the startling prospect of a royal divorce. No sooner had Geoffrey and Henry left Paris than Eleanor obtained Louis' consent for a divorce and the first steps were taken for an annulment of the royal marriage. Eleanor and Louis went for a last trip together to Aquitaine, where a changing of the guard took place as Louis' officers were replaced by Eleanor's own vassals. All was set in order for Eleanor's return to take over the rule of Aquitaine by herself.

Early in the spring of 1152 Eleanor and Louis met at a royal castle near Orléans, where an assembly had been called for the annulment proceedings of the royal marriage. All went smoothly, with witnesses to prove that the couple were fourth cousins, too closely related to be lawfully married. The archbishop solemnly declared the marriage null and void. Eleanor had to accept the decree that her little daughters, Marie and Alix, be awarded to their father. Then Eleanor took leave of Louis, whose only consolation was his conscience and the approval of Abbot Bernard and church friends, who had never approved of Eleanor. The Pope was silent this time.

Eleanor had gained her freedom and independence at last, no small achievement. That a woman would seek and obtain a divorce was unheard of in those times, yet Eleanor had managed it. As a rule only husbands had the right to seek divorces, and a divorced wife, even a queen, was usually packed off to a nunnery or left to pine away, forgotten, in some out-of-the way manor house.

Not Eleanor. Years of unhappiness, frustration, and boredom now lay behind her as she headed home. She was twenty-nine and had never looked more radiantly beautiful.

The countryside was growing green with early spring as she rode south on her palfrey. It was the day before Palm Sunday, and villagers were stripping bark from trees for palms and decorating their house fronts for the next day's procession.

Though Eleanor was happy, she was not safe. News of her divorce had flown before her, alerting bold adventurers of this golden opportunity to waylay the erstwhile queen. When she stopped for the night at a castle near the Loire River, she was warned that the son of her former enemy, the Count of Champagne, was camped nearby, plotting to kidnap her. Eleanor managed to slip out of the castle that night, sending scouts ahead to look for other ambushes. As she neared the River Creuse, she learned that another young knight was lying in wait at the river's ford to capture her and force her to marry him. Eleanor and her escort again managed to outsmart her would-be kidnaper, found another place to ford the river, and sped on to the safety of her old castle in Poitiers.

Within her strong tower she could relax and laugh at her narrow escapes, but she was incensed and indignant that such insignificant young knights would dare attempt to lay hands on a former queen. She saw the need of a husband, one who could wield a sword in her defense. This time she would have a husband of her own choosing.

That Eleanor had already chosen Henry, Duke of Normandy, was her well-kept secret and not yet known to the world. Now she sent a message to him, announcing that she was free.

That Henry was only eighteen and she twenty-nine didn't bother her at all. With his wide experience, his good education, he seemed older than his years. He was, above all, a perfect warrior knight, unafraid and bold, gallant and well-spoken.

That Eleanor and Henry were cousins, as closely related as she and Louis, didn't bother her either. She couldn't have cared less whether her husband was a cousin or not, though it had been a handy excuse to get her divorce. She knew that all kings and queens, dukes and duchesses, counts and countesses—all aristocrats in Europe—were cousins in one degree or another, usually too closely related to marry if Abbot Bernard did the checking into their family trees.

In the month of May, just eight weeks after the divorce, Henry, Duke of Normandy, now also Count of Anjou, came riding over the drawbridge into Eleanor's courtyard. He had a falcon perched on his wrist and, like his father, wore a sprig of broom plant in his cap. Eleanor had never set eyes on Louis before she married him. She had seen Henry only briefly, but long enough to know she wanted him for her husband. It had not been hard for Henry to make up his mind to marry the beautiful Eleanor, whose charm and intelligence would be such an asset to him. That there was a good deal of malicious gossip about her made her all the more interesting.

Aside from being attracted to each other, Eleanor and Henry had many things in common. Both were born to rule, both were ambitious, and both knew the material gains they were bringing each other. Their combined lands—Aquitaine, Normandy, and Anjou—would give them power over most of the land from the English Channel to Spain. And there was another prospect, even more glittering. Through his mother, Henry had a claim to the throne of England. Eleanor might be Queen for a second time. The future looked bright for this couple, so much more suited to each other than Eleanor and Louis had been.

The wedding was small and quiet, with only a few friends and relatives attending. It was best not to advertise the marriage in advance. Both Eleanor and Henry knew that as vassals to King Louis, they had no right to marry without his consent. Once married they had nothing to fear, least of all from Louis. It would take some doing to thwart the combined power of Aquitaine, Anjou, and Normandy.

The news of the marriage exploded like a bombshell in Paris. No one was more stunned than Louis. That Eleanor would remarry someday he had had no doubt, but that she would remarry so soon was not only surprising but insulting; that she would marry the vassal he most feared and disliked was the worst blow of all. He could now see why Henry and his father had been so willing to give up the Vexin land. What good would it do Louis, now that Eleanor and Henry controlled such a formidable expanse of territory? He realized that he had been duped. His Kingdom of France had now shrunk back to almost the small size it had been before his brilliant marriage.

He summoned Henry to appear to answer for his treason, but getting no response, he prepared for war. He charged into Normandy, but Henry, whose uncanny speed confounded all his enemies, came like a whirlwind to counterattack. Within a few weeks the French were routed and Louis fell ill. He retired to his castle on the Seine to brood upon his losses. All Suger's careful work to keep Aquitaine now came undone. The scheming and determination of a beautiful and impetuous woman had changed the balance of power and the boundaries of kingdoms.

V

Waiting for the Crown

For the first time in many years Eleanor was happy. She had cast aside a dull king for a bold young knight, with whom life promised to be anything but boring.

In the autumn following their marriage, Eleanor and Henry took a honeymoon in Aquitaine. Henry could not help but be pleased with what he saw—the lush vineyards, olive orchards, plump grazing sheep, sleek horses, well-stocked hunting grounds, and the best-trained falcons in all Europe. In Bordeaux he cast his practical eye on the merchant ships being loaded with barrels of red wine. He had done well to marry Eleanor.

These sculptured heads may represent Eleanor (on the left) and Henry, and may have been made to commemorate the couple's trip through Aquitaine. Rescued from a ruined church near Bordeaux, they can be seen in the Metropolitan Museum's Cloisters, New York.

The Aquitanians were happy to have their Duchess home again, but they did not feel so kindly toward her husband, a foreigner to them. They mistrusted his authoritarian manner. Henry sensed this hostility and had a hard time keeping his temper. Once he didn't. When some of Eleanor's vassals failed to show him proper respect as their new Duke, he flew into one of his famous black rages, screaming and cursing, kicking and smashing furniture, his eyes red with uncontrollable anger. When his tantrum subsided, he was still resentful and meted out unnecessarily harsh punishments.

If Eleanor was shocked at this behavior, she did not show it or let it mar their happiness. But if she had any secret thoughts of managing this young husband as she had Louis, she soon realized that he was no more to be managed than *she* was.

After this trip Henry felt the time had come to go to England to press his claim to the English throne. In case there was opposition, he took 146 knights and hundreds of archers. He left Eleanor in charge of their combined lands. So many lands and titles! They were now Duke and Duchess of Normandy, Duke and Duchess of Aquitaine, Count and Countess of Anjou, Count and Countess of Poitou. It would have seemed enough to most people, but Henry's ambitions were boundless and so were Eleanor's.

During Henry's absence Eleanor sometimes stayed in his castle in Anjou, sometimes in her own in

Poitiers, both more pleasing to her than the cold, bleak castle in Paris. Eleanor was pregnant but busier than ever, governing in Henry's place, collecting taxes, dispensing justice. As though to prove her new happiness she generously granted charters, giving privileges to towns and churches, the use of forests for firewood, ponds for fishing. She gave freely of her own wealth for building projects. Attached to one gift, she wrote, "with a glad heart . . . now that I am joined in wedlock to Henry, Duke of Normandy."

Eleanor found time to pursue her other interests too. Free from the restraints of Louis' puritanical court, she set about creating a court to her own taste. No one was better equipped than the well-traveled Eleanor to be the center of a refined and cultivated court. She had not forgotten the elegance and luxury, the courtesy and ceremony, in the courts of Constantinople and Antioch. Eleanor wanted a court where music, poetry, and literature could flourish, where good manners and respect for ladies would be observed. She welcomed young knights and the footloose troubadours who had been dismissed from Paris after her divorce. She became a magnet for wandering minstrels and poets who flocked to her court to sing her praises and to take advantage of her generosity.

Among those vying to please the Duchess was a young troubadour, Bernard de Ventadour, whose romantic love songs, in the Provençal dialect of the day, expressed the ideals of chivalry Eleanor was so eager to spread.

Domma, per vostr' amor
Jonh las mas et ador
Gens cors ab frescha color,
Gran mal me faitz traire.

Sweet lady, for your love
With clasped hands, I bless
Your radiance, high above
My deep unhappiness.

In verse after verse Bernard poured out wildly romantic longings for his beautiful, gracious lady, who he knew was far beyond his reach. Whether or not Bernard was really in love with Eleanor, she was his inspiration and patroness, as she was for many other poets and writers.

A whole new life-style and a new romantic literature were beginning at Eleanor's court. Tales of the great hero Charlemagne, which praised only warriors' courage in battle, were giving way to tales of adventure in which women were important. The joy of love was added to the joy of battle. Ancient Celtic stories of King Arthur, his knights, and his Queen Guinevere, sung by bards and handed down from generation to generation, traveled along the pilgrim highways to inns and castles. At Eleanor's court they fired the imaginations of poets, who put them into written verse for the first time—often at Eleanor's request. In these retold Celtic tales the knights no longer battled just for their king but for a lady. They went on long, perilous adventures to prove their valor, loyalty, and love for some beautiful woman. The heroes and heroines of these stories behaved and dressed more like the knights and ladies at Eleanor's court than like their original Celtic counterparts. They expressed Eleanor's ideals of chivalry and longing for romance.

"With clasped hands," a troubadour kneels before his lady love.

Virgin and child (a thirteenth-century sculpture).

As Eleanor was striving to elevate the position of women, the worship of the Virgin Mary was also spreading through the land. Most of the new Gothic cathedrals were dedicated to Notre Dame, Our Lady.

God, the Supreme Judge, was remote from men; Mary, the Mother of God, seemed closer, more understanding and forgiving. The cult of chivalry, invented by and for the nobility, and the cult of the Virgin Mary, popular with the masses, developed separately, but both helped to slowly shed a softening influence on society.

Henry was still in England when Eleanor gave birth to her first son, named William after both her father and Henry's great-grandfather, William the Conqueror. When Henry returned to Normandy, Eleanor and her baby were there to greet him. Henry was overjoyed with this little baby, as he would be with all the seven other children Eleanor was to bear him in the next decade.

Henry added to their joy the good news that his campaigns had been successful—that he had forced the English King Stephen to acknowledge him as the next King of England. Though they would have to wait until Stephen died, the future was full of promise.

While the world was opening up for Eleanor and Henry, Louis' future looked bleaker and bleaker. But after consulting his chaplains, Louis bestirred himself and took a second wife in the desperate hope that he might yet have a son and heir.

While still in Normandy, Eleanor met her new mother-in-law, Matilda, a formidable, outspoken woman, not much loved but sometimes admired for her toughness, intelligence, and courage. She was nothing like Louis' nagging mother but blunt and to the point, with a keen sense of politics. Eleanor could see where Henry got his political sharpness and his unrelenting ambition. Matilda, granddaughter of William the Conqueror, had tried to assert her own right to the English throne, but the English had not been ready for a woman ruler and had chosen her worthless cousin, Stephen, instead. During his weak reign the feudal barons got out of hand—anarchy and civil war devastated the English countryside.

Eleanor and Henry did not have long to wait. Far sooner than expected came the welcome news that King Stephen had died, in the fall of 1154. Few Englishmen regretted his death, and longing for a strong, wise ruler, they eagerly awaited the young Duke and Duchess of Normandy. Henry was just twenty-one and Eleanor thirty-two.

Things were falling into place at a giddy pace. Nothing seemed to stand in the way of this well-matched couple, who could now look forward to ruling over lands that stretched all the way from the borders of Scotland to the borders of Spain.

The news was received in Paris with alarm. That Eleanor had had a son was hard enough for Louis to bear. Now his worst fears had come true.

VI

The Second Crown

The only obstacle that bothered Henry at the moment was the weather. The coast of Normandy was
dark with storms, rain, and sleet; howling winds
churned the English Channel. It seemed that the
skies would never clear as Eleanor and Henry waited
impatiently for a shift in the weather. After a month
Henry could stand it no longer. He had a crown
to claim, and this miserable Channel, less than
a hundred miles across, was holding him up. Defying the stormy seas and gales, he ordered his
fleet to set sail. Calling on God to protect them,
he led Eleanor, now pregnant again and carrying
her little son in her arms, aboard the royal galley.
For more than twenty-four hours the ships were

tossed on the rough Channel waters, their feeble lantern lights lost to each other in the murky dark. But the next day all landed safely, though scattered, on the shores of England.

That Eleanor and Henry had braved such storms at all and had landed successfully seemed a miracle to the English. It was a good omen, and the English were full of admiration and thrilled at the prospect of a king and queen who had such courage and fortitude.

Amidst a cheering, swelling crowd the couple rode to London, where hasty preparations for the coronation in Westminster Abbey had been made. Henry was in a hurry—he was always in a hurry—and the English had no time to renovate the dilapidated abbey church, all but ruined in the recent civil wars. But the ceremony itself was splendid. Henry, usually so careless of his dress, bore himself regally in a magnificent fur-trimmed robe. He was crowned King Henry II of England, but throughout history has been more often known as Henry Plantagenet—a title he passed on to a long line of English kings. Eleanor was crowned for a second time, Queen Eleanor of England. All eyes were riveted on the robust young King and his beautiful wife. The English looked forward to a new era of peace and prosperity.

The nearby royal palace of Westminster was in even worse condition than the abbey, so the King and Queen stayed temporarily across the Thames River in a royal manor house. From here they had a fine view of the crowded city, the imposing Tower of London built by William the Conqueror, and St. Paul's Cathedral, still under construction.

Eleanor found London unlike any city she had ever seen. Perhaps it was the climate and the people that seemed so different. Though London was even colder than Paris, the hearty, red-cheeked people were not bothered by the weather. In the bitter cold of winter Eleanor saw an unusual sight—young men and boys gliding on frozen ponds and marshes, using horses' shinbones strapped to their boots for skates. They propelled themselves swiftly forward by striking poles into the ice. In warm weather, Eleanor could watch another odd sport from London Bridge— boys tilting in small boats. Standing in the prows and holding lances, they sped toward a target, a shield hanging from a pole. If they hit the target and remained standing, they were applauded. More often than not they plunged into the river amid uproarious guffaws from the onlookers.

City life was busiest along the waterfront, where ships loaded and unloaded at the endless rows of docks and wharves. The smell of fish, wool, and beer hung in the foggy air. Shops and drinking taverns lined the streets. The most popular place was a public cookshop near the river, always open and ready with a hot meal day or night, cheap meals of coarse meats and fish for the poor, delicate venison or quail for the rich.

London was as full of merchants as Paris was of students. It had a prosperous look, its men intent on work and business but full of vigor and good

Ships unloading at a river's dock.

cheer. Eleanor found the English more friendly and hospitable than Parisians, but London seemed to her a man's city. She saw no signs of frivolity, no troubadours or wandering minstrels. She realized that London could stand some changes, but she made no complaints. Eleanor was more of a doer than a complainer and there was plenty of time to change things. Right now, with Henry at her side, she was happy and content. Within a few months of their arrival Eleanor had a second son, whom they named Henry.

Soon Eleanor, who bounced back from every

childbirth with her usual vitality and good health, was put to the test of keeping up with her even more energetic husband. Shortly after her second childbirth she was off with Henry on one of his many strenuous trips to check up on his new kingdom. As on travels with her father long ago in Aquitaine, Eleanor and Henry gathered up and took along their entire household—some two hundred persons, including the two babies, and all their belongings. Henry, so restless that he never sat down except to eat a meal or ride a horse, often made things difficult. He refused to stick to any normal routine and acted on sudden impulse. If he ordered his courtiers to be ready to leave at dawn, he might sleep until noon. If he planned to leave at noon, he was sure to be up at sunrise shouting orders to his men, who frantically scurried around, half asleep, trying to load wagons and harness horses.

Despite the pandemonium caused by his sudden changes, Henry did a thorough job of bringing order to England, so scarred by recent warfare. He and Eleanor took note of ruined farms, meadows full of weeds and brambles, forests full of poachers and robbers, deserted villages, and castles leveled almost to the ground.

Lawlessness confronted them everywhere. Eleanor had learned about church law in Paris; now she learned about the laws of the people in England. What a jumble they were! Laws differed from village to village, many people didn't know what land they owned, criminals went unpunished, innocent men were hanged. To find out the guilt or innocence of an accused person, crude, old-fashioned trials by combat or ordeal were still common. It was believed that these showed God's judgment. When a woman was accused of a crime, she had to carry a red-hot iron for three paces. If at the end of three days her burn was at least the size of half a walnut, she was declared guilty. In trial by combat the accused had to fight against his accuser. The loser, if not already dead, was guilty and straightway sent to the gallows. Henry offered a fairer, more logical type of trial: trial by jury, which in those days meant using twelve honest men, who knew the facts and people involved, to swear on the guilt or innocence of the accused. This was a better way to find out the truth and surely closer to God's judgment.

As Henry and Eleanor traveled from town to town, people were invited to bring their complaints directly to the royal court for trial. Seeing the King in person, and often the Queen beside him, gave the people confidence in the King's justice. Henry's trials by jury became popular. The decisions of his courts were used to decide similar cases, and helped make the laws the same throughout England, gradually forming the basis of the English common law.

The royal trips were not all business, and Henry found time to indulge his love of sport, especially hunting. Always afraid of getting fat, he felt the need of strenuous exercise. Though Eleanor loved comfort and luxury, she had no trouble keeping up with Henry when it came to roughing it. Her adventures in the wild mountains while on crusade stood her in good stead now. She often followed

In this painting of a hawking expedition, the King and Queen seem more interested in each other than in their sport. Note the expressions of the horses, who appear to be listening to what their riders are saying.

Henry on horseback into the forests to hunt wild boar, stag, and fox, or went hawking with him along the streams and riverbanks where quail, wild duck, and partridge were plentiful.

Eleanor soon persuaded Henry to have the royal palace of Westminster done over and made livable. Then she refurbished it with her usual taste for elegance, importing tapestries, silk cushions, oil for lamps, and incense. She also imported exotic spices for her kitchen and wines from Bordeaux—she could not stand the heavy English beer. Importing wine became a thriving business. Eleanor owned the dock called Queenhithe, where the wines from Aquitaine were unloaded. Though its elaborate fortified gate and tower are gone, the landing place can still be seen today.

More important for England, she imported her life-style, her interests in the arts, her poets and musicians. She brought the backward island into contact with the new ideas of chivalry and romance from her southern lands. Though churchmen, as they had in Paris, raised their eyebrows at the showy young knights and troubadours who frequented Eleanor's court at Westminster—they feared they might contaminate the stalwart English youth—they could not stop her influence. Even church music showed a change since Eleanor's arrival in London, with choirs singing in strange new harmonies that seemed designed to stir the senses, diverting thoughts away from prayer. Under Eleanor's inspiration and patronage, still other and more fanciful versions of the adventures of King Arthur, his knights, and his beautiful Queen Guinevere, were set in verse and dedicated to her. It is now thought that the fairy-tale Queen Guinevere was modeled after Eleanor herself.

Though Henry did not share Eleanor's enthusiasm for love lyrics, he happily patronized the Arthur stories as good propaganda. He hoped that the people would see in him a second glorious King Arthur, with his wise, strong rule and far-flung conquests, and that these stories would lend a special luster to the English crown. Their popularity spread far and wide. With their enchanted castles, magic, and romance, they provided an escape from the harshness of daily feudal life.

But Eleanor could not long escape her own strenuous feudal obligations—riding from castle to castle throughout the length and breath of England, crossing and recrossing the English Channel, more often than not pregnant. Sometimes Henry left her behind as he dashed to the continent to check his other lands, far more difficult to rule than England. Henry's rapidity of movement astounded the French. "He must fly rather than travel by horseback or boat," wrote an awed admirer. Eleanor had to be speedy, too, for Henry often summoned her to join him at a moment's notice.

When Eleanor was left to rule in Henry's absence, the English found there was more to her than her beauty and interest in the arts. Eleanor had come a long way since her early adolescent years as Queen of France, when she had pushed Louis to many rash deeds to satisfy her whims. She was far more mature now, and she had a real talent for ruling. She was a shrewd politician and able to mete out justice as well as any king. When some monks complained that they had been unjustly deprived of their lands, she acted immediately, ordering the sheriff of London to look into the matter at once. She said that she wanted to hear no more complaints of deficiencies of law and justice, and that she would not tolerate the monks' being deprived of anything that belonged to them.

The words of a poet perhaps describe best what the people thought of their queen:

High-born lady, excellent and valiant,
True, understanding, noble,
Ruled by right and justice,
Queen of beauty and largesse.

With their interest in justice and their patronage of the arts, Eleanor and Henry gave England a great push forward.

VII

Murder in the Cathedral

Into Eleanor's happy, full life there now came an intruder who cast a shadow between her and her husband. This was Thomas Becket, Henry's chancellor—his top advisor and most trusted man. Son of a wealthy London merchant, Becket had been working as a deacon for the Archbishop of Canterbury when Henry summoned him to the chancellorship, a dazzling job for the churchman and more suited to his worldly tastes for luxury and pleasure. Fifteen years older than Henry, Becket immediately cast a spell over the young King, who grew to worship him and consulted him on every move. They became bosom companions in business and pleasure, riding, hunting, hawking together—often leaving Eleanor behind. Henry soon set Becket up in a splendid London mansion, where he lived in sumptuous elegance, serving lavish meals that more than equaled those in the royal palace. The most important dignitaries began going to Becket's house instead of to the palace. Eleanor, so eager to rule along with Henry, often felt left out. Though she could not help admire Becket for his efficiency and ability, she resented his hold over her husband. She sometimes wondered if he was as fond of Henry as Henry was of him. She finally became resigned to Becket and accepted him as an undesirable member of the family. From now on, she realized, he would be in on all their family plans and ambitious schemes for the future.

Henry was fast becoming the most powerful ruler of western Europe but, never satisfied, wanted still more power and more lands. (He had once said to Eleanor that the world would be better off under one strong ruler.) One way to increase their lands, as Eleanor knew only too well, was to marry their children to wealthy potentates. Eleanor was certainly doing her part by steadily increasing the family. Her third child, Matilda, was followed by another son, Richard; then came Geoffrey, Eleanor, Joanna, and last, when she was forty-four years old, John. With her two daughters by Louis, Eleanor had ten children in all, five sons and five daughters. Only one—the first son, William—died in childhood—a remarkable record of health for the Middle Ages.

One piece of land Henry hungered for was that

small but important Vexin borderland that he and his father had given King Louis when they secretly plotted to get the bigger prize of Aquitaine and Eleanor. The Vexin jutted annoyingly into Henry's Duchy of Normandy, and he needed it to straighten out his borders. No doubt he could have taken it by force, but that would have been breaking his vassal's oath; and now that he was a king, Henry would not stoop to that—it would be a bad example to his own vassals. As King and Queen of the English, Henry and Eleanor were absolute rulers of England, but on the continent they were still vassals to the French King. It was an odd situation, and one they hoped to change. They looked forward to a time when their family would hold both the English and French crowns. Naturally they were relieved to hear that Louis' second wife had given birth to another disappointing daughter. They— and Becket too, of course—put their heads together and came up with a bold scheme—a marriage contract between their three-year-old Prince Henry and Louis' six-month-old Princess Marguerite, whose wedding gift, or dowry, would be the Vexin. When little Henry came of age—they liked to think—he would wear the crown of France.

Considering Louis' feeling about Eleanor and Henry, the scheme would need careful, tactful handling. Henry chose Becket to carry out the diplomatic mission, but it was Eleanor who planned the tactics—a great pageant and display of English might and wealth, designed to dazzle the French. Eleanor knew people, and knew that there was nothing like a good show to put everyone in a good humor. With Becket, a good showman himself, in charge of the procession, they had no doubt that their marriage offer would prove irresistible.

People gaped with wonder as the procession, heralded by the blowing of trumpets, approached the gates of Paris. First came two hundred and fifty foot soldiers singing Welsh and English songs, followed by huntsmen leading their hunting hounds on leashes, falconers with hooded hawks perched on their wrists, all in bright new livery. Then came eight large wagons, each drawn by five well-groomed horses and guarded by fierce mastiffs. Each wagon was loaded with rich furnishings of tapestries, silk covers, chests of gold and silver, barrels of English beer and ale. One wagon with gilded wheels and scarlet covering contained a portable chapel for Becket's private use. Twelve pack mules laden with Becket's table settings of goblets and gold plate, his linen and clothing, came next; cavorting on the back of each mule was a long-tailed monkey, a novel sight for the French. Then came knights in shining armor, riding huge war-horses and holding aloft the royal English banners with their golden lions, their squires walking beside them, carrying their shields. And last, after bishops and officers of the royal household, came Becket himself, the most magnificent of all in brocaded velvet, astride his horse, whose trappings were of silver and gold. "If such be only the Chancellor," the

An elegant carriage such as Becket may have used for his great procession.

people cried, "what must be the King?"

Even King Louis was impressed and outdid himself in hospitality. Then Becket, in turn, outdid the King with a lavish banquet for a thousand people. With unequaled generosity he gave away prized falcons, hunting hounds, and well-bred horses. He distributed beer and ale, even gold and silver pieces, throughout the city of Paris. It was the greatest show of the century, and people talked of it for years afterward.

Eleanor had been right: Her show and Becket's showmanship turned out to be a great diplomatic triumph. Louis agreed to engage his little princess to the English Prince and to give up the Vexin when the children were old enough to marry. Then, according to the custom, little Marguerite was handed over to be brought up by her future in-laws. But Louis made one condition—that Eleanor herself have no part in her upbringing.

With that settled, Eleanor went to England while Henry lingered in Normandy. Once more Eleanor

was on the road, going from castle to castle, from town to town, from monastery to monastery. This was the only way a ruler could find out what was going on and keep in touch with the people. It was important, too, to collect the taxes—wool, tin, and flour—due at certain times of year. Though Eleanor always missed Aquitaine, she enjoyed the beauty of England in the spring. She still preferred riding horseback to using horsedrawn carts—without any springs and with their solid wooden wheels, they joggled her unmercifully on the muddy, rutty roads. Riding past bright-green meadows and clear, running streams, she often heard the songs of nightingales and larks. In the villages, with their whitewashed, thatched cottages, she paused to greet the villagers who thronged the road to see her pass. In the distance she could see the white spire of some abbey or the hilltop castle where she would be welcomed for the night.

Her travels were cut short by a summons from Henry to hasten back to Normandy and bring their

Village peasants tend their animals, which often shared their cottages.

little Prince. Henry had heard that King Louis' second wife had died in giving birth to still another daughter. In something of a panic he had married a third wife. Louis might still have a son and undo all Henry's plans for the future. Better marry his little son to the French Princess right away, lest Louis change his mind. Without alerting the French, Henry and Eleanor had their five-year-old Prince Henry married to the three-year-old Princess Marguerite. No sooner was the ceremony ended than King Henry dashed off to claim Marguerite's wedding gift, the Vexin land. Once again Louis had been duped by the crafty English King.

With the Vexin, Henry had rounded out his borders on the continent; his lion banners floated defiantly from towers all along his frontiers. An interlude of peace now gave Eleanor and Henry a chance to use their wealth to spread the arts and learning, to build and rebuild castles, churches, and monasteries. In Eleanor's beloved Poitiers they built new city walls and bridges and laid the cornerstone of a new cathedral, St. Peter's. They added a spacious hall to her family castle and filled it with large, arcaded windows opening to views of distant blue hills, a green valley below, and the little River Clain, which, like a moat, almost encircled the town. Near the river was the ancient church of Poitiers' much-loved patron saint, Radegonde. As a child Eleanor had often ridden down from her high castle to attend this church. In the dark crypt beneath the altar, she had placed lighted candles by Saint Radegonde's tomb. Eleanor never tired of the story of the brave and saintly Radegonde, who had been forced against her will to marry a brutal barbarian king of the Franks, long ago in the Dark Ages. When the King murdered her brother, Queen Radegonde fled her fiendish husband. Miraculously protected by God, she took refuge in Poitiers, founded a convent, and devoted her life to the care of the poor and the sick. It seems likely that Radegonde's having the courage to give up a crown and an undesirable husband made a deep impression on Eleanor.

From her castle tower Eleanor could see the enchanting little church, Notre-Dame-la-Grande, now her favorite. Like an ornately carved jewel box, its new façade was encrusted with delicate sculptures, its interior bright with painted frescoes and decorated columns. It was not like any other church, and reminded Eleanor of some of the Moslem architecture she had seen in Antioch.

Henry and Eleanor were so busy with various projects that they had little time to spend with their children. Though Henry was always overjoyed with each new infant, he was not a good father, spoiling his children with gifts of money, titles, and lands but giving them no responsibilities. He was more interested in using them to increase his own power through marriage contracts than in training them for statehood. If not the ideal mother, Eleanor was closer to her children and had more influence on them.

She and Henry knew that it was time for the young prince, aged seven, to have a tutor; but when Henry chose Becket for the job, Eleanor was not pleased. She suffered inwardly as she watched her little son fall like his father under Becket's spell.

Much as Eleanor loved and admired Henry, she noticed more and more that he made mistakes in handling his family.

And now Henry made the greatest mistake of his life. The Archbishop of Canterbury died and Henry chose Becket to fill his place, the highest position of the church in England, and next to the king's the most important. People, used to seeing Becket parading around in silk brocades, hosting sumptuous feasts, or riding to the hunt, were taken aback at this choice. But Henry thought it brilliant—he would use Becket in a double role as both chancellor and archbishop. Through his close friend, who was always willing and able to carry out his every wish, Henry expected to control both church and state.

Becket warned the King that this would lead to trouble and might end their friendship. How could he serve both God and the King equally well? He accepted the job nonetheless and was consecrated into the holy office within a month.

When Eleanor and Henry next saw Becket he was a changed man. Gone were his showy clothes. In their place he wore a coarse black robe. Henry could see that Becket was no longer a fit companion for hunting or hawking, and much to the King's annoyance, Becket resigned his job as chancellor. It was obvious that his former friend was shifting his loyalty from the King to the church. Difficult as it was for Henry to accept, Becket became wholeheartedly dedicated to God, the Pope, and the church. Soon the old friends were quarreling. As Eleanor could not manage Henry, so Henry could no longer manage Becket.

Henry had hoped to use Becket to correct abuses in the church law. It was well known that there were robbers and even murderers among the lower, more ignorant clergy. When tried in church courts they received only mild punishments. Henry felt that they should get the same trials and punishments as all other Englishmen. Becket disagreed, and refused to tamper with church law. At all costs he would uphold the independence of the church and keep it from slipping into Henry's control.

Neither Becket nor Henry would give an inch, and the quarrel grew bigger and bigger. When Becket forbade his clergy to obey any of Henry's reforms, the King flew into a rage. Becket finally fled England to escape the King's fury and took refuge with King Louis, ever ready to defend a churchman, especially one quarreling with the English King.

The quarrel went on for years. Attempts to make up always ended in failure, for each man now sought to ruin the other. When Henry had his son crowned as the future King of England by another archbishop in 1170, Becket was so angry that he excommunicated all who had taken part in the coronation. As head of the church in England, only he had the power to crown kings. He returned to Canterbury to assert that power.

Henry and Eleanor were holding Christmas court in Normandy that winter when Henry got the news of Becket's latest defiance. He flew into one of his blackest rages and, in a torrent of angry words, was heard to say, "Will no one rid me of this troublesome, lowborn priest?" Four loyal knights slipped away, crossed the Channel, and sped to Canterbury. They entered the cathedral, shouting, "Where is Thomas Becket, traitor to the King?" They found him praying by the altar and threatened him with death if he did not repent his treason. When Becket refused to yield, the hotheaded knights surrounded him and drew their swords. A blade flashed as it struck at Becket's head. Then came a second blow, then a third, which severed his head; his body crumpled to the foot of the altar. While the assassins fled into the night, the Archbishop's blood—the red blood of martyrdom—slowly spread over the white marble paving. Thunder and lightning, out of season, rent the sky, announcing the terrible murder in the cathedral.

Almost immediately miracles were reported at the scene of the murder, and Becket dead became more powerful than he had ever been in life. Within two years he was made a saint, and his tomb became the most popular shrine in all England. Year in and year out the roads to Canterbury were filled with pilgrims heading toward the holy martyr's shrine, seeking cures and miracles.

The entire Christian world was rocked by the news of the Archbishop's murder in the cathedral. Henry himself was stricken with grief, horrified that his angry words had led to the murder of his former friend. Calling for sackcloth and ashes, he shut him-

The murder of Thomas Becket at Canterbury Cathedral. This thirteenth-century depiction doesn't quite convey the horror of the deed.

self up in his castle, refusing to eat, refusing to see anyone.

Though Henry insisted that he had had no part in or desire for Becket's death, not all believed him. He began to lose his popularity and respect. Only after undergoing penance was he accepted back into the Christian fold. Stripped to the waist, he kneeled on the steps of the cathedral while black-robed monks lashed his bare back again and again with heavy thonged whips.

VIII

Betrayed

Eleanor had stayed aloof from the Becket quarrel, which had dragged on for six stormy years to its tragic end. Though she disliked Becket, she did not think Henry all in the right, and she refused to take sides. She could tell that the quarrel was hurting her husband as she watched his love for Becket turn to hate, his temper tantrums increase—in his worst rages he rolled on the floor and chewed the straw rushes—and his popularity slip. At the same time her ex-husband, Louis, by defending Becket and the church, was gaining prestige.

Shortly after Becket took refuge with King Louis, an unexpected event gave the French great cause for rejoicing and hope for the future. On a hot August night in 1165, a sudden clamor of church bells broke the midnight silence in Paris, bonfires flared in the streets and a cry went up, "By the grace of Heaven, there is born to us tonight a prince who shall be a Hammer to the English." King Louis' prayers had been answered at last, and the French went wild with joy. The prince was named Philip, and with his birth Eleanor's and Henry's plans to gain the throne of France were dashed.

As the future was brightening for her ex-husband King Louis, it was beginning to cloud over for Eleanor. A rift between the couple began when Eleanor came to realize that Henry no longer loved her. Becket's intrusion into their married life had bothered Eleanor, but it was nothing compared to the intrusion of a young, flaxen-haired beauty named Rosamond Clifford, known to the world as Fair Rosamond.

Eleanor had long been aware that Henry enjoyed the company of many other women besides herself—husbands and fathers locked away their wives and daughters when the King was in the neighborhood—but they had been mere passing fancies. There was something different, something serious, about Henry's affair with Rosamond which deeply offended and threatened Eleanor. Henry made no secret of this love and shamelessly flaunted his mistress before the public, setting her up in many of the favorite royal castles.

Eleanor was in England, on her way to Oxford to have her last child, when she learned that Rosamond was installed in the nearby castle of Wood-stock. This had been Eleanor's and Henry's most loved English country estate, where they had spent many happy times and where they had done much to embellish the apartments and the lovely game park. Now Rosamond was living like a queen in Eleanor's own rooms.

In anger and in shame, feeling lonely and ne-glected, Eleanor gave birth to her last child, John, on Christmas Eve, 1166. It is not surprising that he was her least-loved child. After fourteen years of shared hopes and plans, years during which she and Henry saw eye to eye; after all the children she had borne to him; after her devoted support, her dash-ing back and forth across the Channel so many times to help him, Eleanor now felt betrayed. Another terrible thought crossed her mind. If Rosamond should have children, would they supplant her own?

There are many legends of Eleanor's vicious at-tempts to do away with her rival, but no evidence that any one of them is true. She had a better idea. Her revenge was directed not at Rosamond, whom she did not blame—few young girls could resist the advances of a king—but on Henry himself. She knew the grasping nature of her sons and that she could count on them for help. Now growing to manhood, they were already disgruntled that their father gave them no real power, only empty titles and promises. They were champing at the bit to rule the lands assigned them—Normandy and Anjou to Prince Henry, Aquitaine to Richard, Brittany to Geoffrey.

But Eleanor knew that Henry never meant to give their sons any real power as long as he lived. Henceforth Eleanor would back her three older sons to gain their rights, even to rebellion against their father. Thus would she strike at Henry where it would hurt him most—his lust for power.

Though Henry no longer loved his wife, he still needed her at times. He had been trying to stamp out rebellions among the Aquitanians, who despised their foreign king from the north. He had scaled the heights of redoubtable castles, razed their walls, and ravaged their farms, but no sooner had he quelled one uprising than another started up. Perhaps, he thought, Eleanor could better manage her own unruly vassals while he went back to England. When he summoned his wife to Aquitaine, she was already planning to go there. She would certainly not stay in England to play second to Henry's mistress. She packed up all her belongings, planning never to return. Henry could go his way and she would go back to Aquitaine, where, as Duchess long ago, she had been treated as a queen.

Eleanor found her duchy anything but peaceful, still smoldering from Henry's harsh treatment. While she and her small escort of knights were riding toward her castle in Poitiers, they ran into an ambush of angry Aquitanians seeking revenge for Henry's destruction of their lands, hoping to capture the Queen and hold her for a high ransom in order to recoup their losses. Eleanor, who had escaped the clutches of brigands before, galloped swiftly to safety, while her knights protected her flight and battled the attackers. Soon only one knight, William Marshal, was left to fight on alone. When his horse was killed beneath him, he set his back to a hedge and fought off his assailants, "like a wild boar besieged by hounds," until a lance thrust from behind the hedge pierced his thigh. He was taken prisoner and held for ransom. Eleanor soon heard of his bravery in her behalf, paid the ransom, gave him a new horse and armor, and welcomed him to her castle. He became her knight-in-arms and a devoted companion to her sons, teaching them knightly skills and tournament play. William Marshal was an example of a perfect knight, loyal and true to Eleanor's family for the rest of his life.

Eleanor gradually restored some measure of peace and order to her duchy, using persuasion where Henry had used force. She undid some of Henry's oppressive rules, recalled exiled vassals, and revived old customs, fairs, and festivals, to please her people. She threw herself with enthusiasm into ruling her own lands, hoping to cut Aquitaine off from Henry's empire, to make it independent as it had been long before she had had any husbands. Eleanor, now forty-five, was through with husbands. From now on her obligations would be to her children and her land, where she would be the mistress.

IX

Courts of Love

Though Eleanor and Henry were not formally separated, they no longer lived together and met only occasionally for business or family affairs. Henry, somewhat disgraced by the Becket affair, was by no means subdued. He had thought it wise to get away until the shock of Becket's murder blew over; he had gone far north to campaign in Ireland. Though he only conquered a small part of the island, he had sown the seeds of Irish hatred for the English that still exists today.

In taking up her career of ruling Aquitaine, Eleanor was eager to have her son Richard recognized as her heir, the future Duke of Aquitaine. She wanted to impress upon her people that he, not King Henry, would be her co-ruler and that he, not Henry, would be the rightful heir after she died. She took Richard to the far corners of her duchy to show him off, and she had him crowned Duke of Aquitaine with as much ceremony as a royal coronation. Eleanor doted on this handsome, talented son, who in his early teens was already tall and powerfully built. He had his father's ruddy cheeks but darker, auburn hair. Most talented and intelligent of her sons, he also had his mother's love of art, poetry, and music. Like Eleanor's troubadour grandfather, he composed music and verse. Eleanor at last had someone she could mold into her ideal knight—and she did more, besides: She taught him the arts of statecraft.

Though Eleanor had to be on the road much of the time, she made Poitiers her home base. This was no thick-walled fortress like most castles in England, with their drafty, smoke-filled rooms, full of hunting hounds and littered rushes. This was an elegant castle fit for a queen. The sun poured into the great hall through the new arcaded windows all day long, and the adjacent tower had comfortable rooms with privacy for women.

Eleanor had a huge household to cope with, and her castle swarmed with young people—knights, ladies-in-waiting, adolescents, and small children. There were her own handsome sons and beautiful daughters; her daughter-in-law, Marguerite; and future daughters-in-law: Constance of Brittany, engaged to young Geoffrey, and Alais of France, engaged to Richard (an arrangement he later rejected).

In a castle courtyard—much like Eleanor's—young people gather to sing and talk of love.

Her ten-year-old Matilda had just gone off to Germany, where she would later marry the Duke of Saxony; her namesake Eleanor would soon go to Spain to marry the King of Castile; and little Joanna was engaged to the future King of Sicily. Through this web of entangling alliances Eleanor's and Henry's descendants would provide no end of kings and queens of Europe, as well as one German emperor and one saint. The only member of the family not yet provided for was baby John, who was therefore jokingly nicknamed John Lackland, a nickname he never learned to like. It was an odd assortment of young people, with children of Eleanor's two husbands—one divorced, the other estranged—mingling together along with their southern cousins and relatives.

Besides this extended family there came a steady stream of troubadours and entertainers glad to have their patroness back. From time to time there also came highborn young men and women eager to join the gay social life in Poitiers. The aristocratic young Aquitanian knights, always an unruly lot, had been so long without a steady ruler—ever since Eleanor had left to be Queen of France thirty years before— that they were more out of control than ever. Crusades had been an outlet for their youthful energies, but in peacetime these footloose knights—especially the younger sons who had no titles or settled futures—became a menace. Jobless and restless, they roamed the land in search of trouble and daredevil adventure.

There was, however, one substitute for war: that popular medieval sport, the tournament. Spring was the time for tournaments as it was for fairs and religious festivals. From Easter until mid-June the highways were jammed with knights and squires, horse dealers, armorers, and wandering minstrels, making the tournament circuit. Unlike later tournaments, where knights encased in plated armor jousted in single combat before grandstand audiences, tournaments in Eleanor's day were really minibattles. At the blast of a herald's trumpet, the mail-clad knights astride their huge war-horses leveled their lances and dashed pell-mell against opposing knights. When lances broke, swords were drawn to continue the battle. Fortunes were won and lost on these fields of battle. Though the object was to capture, not kill, opponents—the victor won the horse and arms of his captive and could hold him for ransom—there were many cracked skulls, and many young knights lay dead on the field at the end of the day.

Eleanor's oldest son, Prince Henry, had a passion for tournaments and adventure. He and his tutor-in-arms, William Marshal, the gallant knight errant who had saved Eleanor from kidnapers, made the rounds of tournaments every spring. William had already won fame and made a considerable fortune through his jousting skills. He often gave his earnings to help bail the Prince out of debt—the handsome, lovable Prince was generous to the point of being a spendthrift. He was the idol of the tournament crowd and always had a large following of wild, dissolute young knights, eager to cash in on his generosity and to follow him to tournaments or on other crazy escapades. Once, after a tournament, he thought it would be fun to invite all the young men with the name of his companion-in-arms, William, to a feast. One hundred and seventeen young Williams showed up, and he wined and dined them lavishly. His extravagance annoyed his father no end. He annoyed his mother, too, when he and his friends arrived at her castle straight from a tournament, streaked with blood and dirt and smelling of horses. Eleanor refused to let them in until they had washed and tidied up. It was not that Eleanor disapproved of tournaments. She didn't. She knew that they helped train warriors in courage and skill. She was proud of Richard, who had already passed one test in training for knighthood—being able to run, fully clad in chain mail, and leap onto a horse without using the stirrups. But prowess was only one knightly virtue she admired. She insisted on cleanliness and manners too.

Eleanor needed help to train and discipline these spirited young people, all under the age of twenty. Strangely enough, the person who came to help her was her first child, Marie, born to her and Louis long ago. (Perhaps Louis thought it wise to have Marie in Poitiers to check up on his young daughter, Marguerite, married to Prince Henry.) Eleanor had not seen Marie for eighteen years, and both rejoiced in the reunion. Now Countess of Champagne, Marie was in her late twenties and had two children of her own. Brought up in the strict schooling of Paris, she nonetheless blossomed under her mother's influence and soon warmed to the more lenient southern way of life. She responded, like her half-brother

Richard, to the beauties of lyric poetry and music. She, Richard, and their mother had much in common and were always devoted to each other.

Eleanor and Marie began to school the boisterous youth in courtly behavior, especially manners and respect for women. They devised a sort of parlor game based on the popular subject sung about by every troubadour—love. The name of the game was Courtly Love, its object to outlaw boorishness and to put women on a pedestal. It aimed to teach young men the art of making love in a refined and civilized way.

Eleanor and Marie knew well enough that women in the real feudal world were still nothing but male property, but in Eleanor's court the real world was turned upside down, into a dream world where men paid homage not to an overlord, but to some fair damsel. As the troubadour Bernard de Ventadour wrote,

Lady, I'm yours and yours shall be
Vowed to your service constantly,
This is the oath of fealty
I pledged to you this long time past.
As my first joy was all in you,
So shall my last be found there too,
So long as life in me shall last.

The game of courtly love was played out in mock trials in which Eleanor and her ladies, as jurors, handed down decisions on the behavior of a lover, using the legal methods the Queen had learned from

Henry. The women, sometimes sixty strong, sat on the raised dais at the end of Eleanor's great hall, while the young men gathered below. The men were well groomed, some of them dressed in such finery that a northern monk complained of their showy cloaks with long flowing sleeves like women's and, worst of all, of their "affecting long hair and shoes with pointed toes."

Before the court came to order, troubadours sang their love songs to the accompaniment of music, minstrels recited tales of King Arthur and his knights. In a new, popular romance, written at the request of Countess Marie, the gallant knight Sir Lancelot underwent appalling ordeals in order to prove his love for Queen Guinevere. The audience must have gasped listening to the minstrel describe Lancelot crossing over the Sword Bridge—a single long blade, cutting edge up—into the mysterious land of Gorre where his beloved Guinevere was held captive. Later in the tale came a moment of almost unbearable suspense when Queen Guinevere put the hero through a most humiliating test of his love for her: In the midst of a tournament, as Lancelot, the greatest and most courageous of King Arthur's knights, was winning victory after victory, he was suddenly ordered by the Queen to do his worst—to play the coward. Suspense mounted as Lancelot, humbly obeying his queen, retreated in fear, was unhorsed and laughed at for his cowardice. Only when the Queen realized that Lancelot had proved his love for her, and ordered him to be himself again and

Lancelot crossing the Sword Bridge to rescue Guinevere from the tower.

to do his best, could the audience relax. Then they could applaud Lancelot's final, unsurpassed victory as he mowed down one foe after another. The women were, of course, pleased that Queen Guinevere had shown such power over her lover. Another popular tale was the tragic romance of Tristan and the Fair Isolde, which was sure to bring tears to all.

Countess Marie also requested a friend to write a guidebook on the art of making love, with rules for the behavior of a young lover toward his loved one, and to explain how true love improved and ennobled a man. "O what a noble thing is love, which makes a man shine with so many virtues, and teaches everyone . . . so many good traits of character." This early how-to book also contained records of twenty-one cases on which the ladies passed judgment.

When the court came to order, young lovers presented their problems or questions to the ladies on the dais. One particular case caused quite a stir. A young knight asked if there could be true love in marriage. After deliberation, Countess Marie handed down the decision that it was unlikely that true, pure love could exist in marriage, since marriage was a commercial contract which united fortunes and lands, not people in love. Marriage was based on obligation and a wife's obedience, and prevented love from being given freely as ideal love ought to be. Eleanor, as the oldest and most experienced woman, was asked to add her opinion. Though she thought it would be admirable if one could find true love in marriage, she reluctantly agreed with the court's decision. She did not say out loud how disillusioned she had been in her own two marriages.

The pure, ideal love that Eleanor and her ladies longed for was not just the satisfaction of sexual lust but something more precious and enduring, something more beautiful—a goal for which a lover must prove himself worthy through good behavior, loyalty, and respect for the woman he loved.

Beyond the walls of Eleanor's castle the real world went on much the same as it always had, with men continuing to treat women as the inferior sex. (One husband got so angry at a troubadour singing ardent love songs to his wife that he had the young man's tongue cut out!) And in spite of the growing

Lady jurors judging cases of young lovers in a mock trial.

cult of the Virgin Mary, the church still considered most women a necessary evil, only useful for continuing the human race. But Eleanor and her ladies had the satisfaction of expressing something new and unconventional, a feminist revolt against male supremacy. In Eleanor's court women were superior to men. They ruled supreme, and like goddesses inspired young men to serve them and adore them.

Though courtly love was largely romantic fantasy expressing what women wanted society to be, not what it really was, it had some influence. Eleanor and her ladies couldn't change the feudal world overnight, but the vogue of courtly love spread throughout aristocratic circles all over Europe, and with it was born the idea of a gentleman. Modern manners owe much to Eleanor's courts of love. We can thank her for the fact that "ladies go first," that some men stand up when women enter a room. Eleanor would be pleased to know that the word "obey" is no longer required of a bride in a wedding ceremony and that her ideal of romantic love, freely given by both man and woman, is now the ideal in marriage.

X

Rebellion

Far away in Ireland, Henry knew nothing of Eleanor's courts of love. He would have laughed at such nonsense as ideal love and lovers pining for fair damsels. In his code women served men, not the other way round. But Henry would not have laughed at everything that went on in Eleanor's castle. Disturbing things were brewing on the fringes of her courtly gatherings.

After the parlor game was over, the young moved out to the courtyard. In the fading light of the warm evening, they clustered in groups to talk—no longer of love, but of politics: of Thomas Becket's murder, of King Henry's disgrace, of whether he really was to blame for the terrible crime. Henry's sons' image of their father had been somewhat shattered by Becket's murder and by his scandalous affair with Fair Rosamond, which had so offended their mother. These recent events added fuel to the sons' already existing complaints against their father. To them he had always been a strange, remote figure with a terrible temper who made sudden, brief appearances, dangled promises, offered gifts, then vanished as quickly as he had come. Eleanor had never been able to make him realize that sons do grow up—Prince Henry was seventeen (two years older than Eleanor had been when she was crowned Queen of France), Richard fifteen, and Geoffrey fourteen—and that they needed responsibility, not coddling. How could they ever learn to rule unless given half a chance?

Of the three older sons, young Henry suffered the most from his overbearing father. He had been promised the most but seemed to have the least. There was his younger brother Richard, already learning to rule Aquitaine with his mother's help, while he, crowned as the future King of England, had not an ounce of power, not even the rule of his small County of Anjou. Even young Geoffrey was recognized as Count of Britanny while he, the Prince, felt he had no recognition at all.

The sons' resentment of their father was rising to a boiling point, and there was no more fertile ground than Poitiers to feed it. Rebellion was second nature to young Aquitanian knights who themselves resented the harsh rule of their foreign

King Henry. They were ready to rebel at a moment's notice. As darkness fell on the castle courtyard, conspiracies were being hatched. Richard could be heard to joke about himself and his family—"from the Devil they came, to the Devil they will go."

In the background was Eleanor, supporting her sons, egging them on to press for their rights, to claim their inheritances. She knew that her ex-husband, Louis, would welcome and aid her sons against his old enemy, Henry. She planned to make her sons' vassal oaths of allegiance to their overlord, the French King, more important than their obedience to their father. Slowly Eleanor and her sons were being drawn into a strange new friendship with her first husband.

Finally word reached Henry in Ireland of trouble brewing in Poitiers—along with a lot of nonsense of courtly love, serious plots were being hatched, odd new alliances being formed. He was not too concerned, for he could not believe that his sons were capable of organizing any serious uprising. After all, they were mere striplings. No doubt they were being corrupted in Eleanor's court and being filled full of ridiculous ideas of romance. He would have a talk with them, confident that he could straighten them out.

After his return to the continent he arranged a family gathering, but it soon turned into a family brawl. Eleanor argued in her sons' behalf, telling Henry to stop treating them as infants, as though they were still in swaddling clothes. Then, when

Henry presented new schemes for his sons' inheritances, they violently objected. And when he proposed providing for little four-year-old John Lackland, by giving him not only Ireland but also strategic castles from each of the older boys' lands, pandemonium broke loose. Prince Henry exploded in a rage worthy of his father. In no way would he give up his border strongholds to that little brat John while he remained a prince without power. Eleanor, Richard, and Geoffrey agreed with the outraged Prince. All flatly refused to go along with Henry's juggling of their lands. Not used to having his will opposed, the King went ahead anyway with his plans. Before the meeting broke up, someone whispered to him that he'd better keep an eye on the Queen; that she was the source of all his trouble with his sons.

The King, however, decided to deal with young Henry first of all. He would keep a close watch on this son and try to get him in hand. He was convinced that his son's dissolute companions were a bad influence, and he sent them all packing. Then he took the resentful Prince to his hilltop castle of Chinon, never letting him out of his sight. Father and son slept in the same bedroom. But when the King woke up one morning, Prince Henry was gone, the drawbridge lowered. The King smelled treachery and went in hot pursuit, but it was too late— young Henry had crossed into the Kingdom of France and taken refuge with King Louis. It must have all been secretly and well planned beforehand. Henry

Henry's great castle of Chinon, overlooking the Vienne River, is depicted in this nineteenth-century engraving.

then found that Richard and Geoffrey were also on their way to Paris, where their overlord, Louis, was waiting to help them, waiting to give the signal for a widespread rebellion against the English King. Their plan was a bold one—to set Prince Henry on the throne of England in the old King's place! Already people were calling the Prince the Young King.

The rebellion broke in the summer of 1173 and spread like wildfire on the continent, then to England, where discontented barons joined the cause and the King of Scotland, seeing his chance, prepared to invade the north of England.

Beset on all sides and short on vassal knights, many of whom had deserted to the Prince, Henry hired mercenaries—a practice much frowned upon by the nobility. He dipped into the royal treasury, kept in the castle of Chinon, and even sold his jeweled sword of state to pay them.

King Louis and Prince Henry first attacked Normandy, but as usual, Louis' plans were clumsy— he was still no match in the game of war against the shrewd English King, and he had no mercenaries. After forty days of fighting (the length of time required of vassal knights to fight for their overlords) Louis and young Henry retreated while King Henry stamped out, one by one, the fires of rebellion.

Before going to England to cope with the rebels there, Henry had to deal with his Queen in Poitiers. One of his still faithful churchmen wrote a letter for him, appealing to Eleanor to put an end to the unnatural strife of sons fighting against their father and to return to her wifely duty. "Return, O illustrious Queen, to your husband, whom you must obey and with whom it is your duty to live," and adding threats of punishment if she refused.

Eleanor had been alarmed at the news from the north—at Louis' bungling and Henry's speedy successes—but she had no intention of returning to her husband. She did not answer the letter, though she knew she was in a dangerous position. Would Henry now descend on Poitiers with his band of tough mercenaries? Her only chance of safety was to join her sons in Paris, beyond the reach of Henry's authority.

When Henry got no response from his wife, he flew into one of his rages and immediately left his post in Normandy to head south. He and his band of mercenaries stormed every rebel castle and town on the way, leaving them in smoldering ruins. The smell of battle came closer and closer to Poitiers.

Only at the last minute had Eleanor been persuaded to leave her castle. Even so she was speedier than Henry this time. When he arrived in Poitiers, the Queen was nowhere to be found. She was fleeing as fast as she could toward the Kingdom of France.

As dusk was falling, some of Henry's scouts spied a small party of knights entering a forest near the French border. Arresting them in the King's name, the scouts found, to their amazement, Queen Eleanor among the group. She was disguised as a knight and riding astride a huge war-horse! After sending word to King Henry, they bore her, prisoner, to the strong castle of Chinon, high above the Vienne River. The heavy portcullis was lowered, the drawbridge raised. Then silence fell. Neither family nor friends knew where she was. Within Chinon's thick walls Eleanor faced the cold reality of the feudal world—she was indeed nothing but her husband's property.

After seeing to his wife's security and knowing that she was safe from further mischief for the moment, Henry returned to Poitiers, the seat of the rebellion. He routed out the remnants of the rebels, as well as the ladies and troubadours who had lingered there. The great hall where Eleanor and her ladies had laid down the rules of courtly love and chivalry was emptied. Countess Marie went home, the troubadours dispersed. The music stopped and a quiet gloom descended on Eleanor's ancestral castle, where women's dreams of ideal love had burned so brightly, if briefly.

With Poitiers silenced and Aquitaine subdued, Henry dashed north to the Channel seaport, Barfleur, where he had ordered the Queen conveyed under guard and put aboard ship. As usual the Channel churned with stormy seas. Eleanor knew that weather never stopped Henry. She could remember how, twenty years earlier, she and Henry had defied the stormy weather in their first triumphant crossing when they had had a crown to gain. There was no triumph to look forward to now— Eleanor was being taken to England as a prisoner. She would pay dearly for her part in their sons' rebellion.

Shouting to God to protect his fleet—Henry's words to God always sounded more like a threat than a prayer—Henry gave orders to sail. The royal galleys rode out the storm and sailed into Southampton with the evening tide. Eleanor was singled out from the group and taken to the confinement of Salisbury Castle.

XI

Prisoner

On a small rise in the middle of Salisbury Plain in southern England stood a formidable castle protected by a double row of walls and a wide, deep moat. Within its thick-walled central tower Eleanor was left to muse upon her past and wonder about her future.

She was not treated like an ordinary criminal, locked in a cell, but was free to move about the castle and its courtyard. As a royal prisoner she was what we might call under house arrest, but she was always well guarded and had no chance of escape. She, who had helped shape world events, now had to rely on her guards for news of the world. She, who had been the magnet of poets and writers, the patroness of art and learning, was now cut off from friends and family and all that she had loved.

While Eleanor adjusted to her new life, Henry was busy stamping out the last fires of rebellion. With his clever military tactics, his incredible speed, and his prompt punishment of the rebels, he soon had all his lands once more under control. Recognized as Lord of Ireland, King of England, Duke and Count of his various continental lands, he seemed to be more powerful than ever. Now he could turn his attention to the Queen.

What to do with his difficult wife? He didn't quite know. She was out of harm's way for the moment, but he knew that she would soon be the object of intrigues, the inspiration for plots and conspiracies. Already one of her Aquitanian admirers had written, "Return, O captive, if you can. . . . The King of the north holds you in captivity. But do not despair; lift your voice like a trumpet and it shall reach the ears of your sons. The day will come when they will set you free and you shall come again to dwell in your native land."

Henry wanted to divorce Eleanor, but that would be repeating Louis' blunder and he would lose his biggest and richest domain, Aquitaine. He then thought of putting her into a nunnery. He knew the perfect place: the Abbey of Fontevrault, where some of Eleanor's forbears had ended their days and which Eleanor had long supported. He knew that Eleanor approved of this most unusual abbey, which housed monks as well as nuns and yet had always been run by a woman, an abbess. Henry thought he could arrange to have Eleanor made Abbess of Fontevrault. That seemed the best solution.

But Eleanor would have none of it. At fifty-three she had no desire to retire to a cloistered life, which she knew would end any hope of future freedom. She appealed to an archbishop, who agreed with Eleanor that the religious life was not for her. He knew as well as Eleanor—and as Henry should have too—that the black headdress of an abbess would not sit on Eleanor's head as becomingly as a queen's crown. And so Henry left her in Salisbury Castle for the moment. But the moment dragged into years—fifteen long years. During all this time Eleanor kept up her courage and her hope, and she learned something that did not come naturally to her: patience.

Eleanor had been in prison two years when she was allowed—under guard, of course—to visit her youngest daughter, Joanna, in Winchester Castle. Eleanor helped eleven-year-old Joanna pack her belongings in preparation for her long trip south to meet her future husband, King William of Sicily.

Eleanor was back in the confinement of Salisbury Castle when Henry's mistress, Fair Rosamond, died of tuberculosis. Though Rosamond had died a natural death while Eleanor was still a well-guarded prisoner, malicious gossipers would delight in far-fetched tales that the Queen had poisoned her.

More important to the feudal world was the death of Eleanor's first husband, Louis, in 1180. The timid King was highly praised for his piety, his good works, and his gentleness. As one devoted chronicler pointed out, his French royal banners bore white lilies, not the fierce lions or leopards the Plantagenets liked to display. But Louis' successor, sixteen-year-old Philip, was made of sterner stuff. Would he be a Hammer to the English, as the French had predicted at his birth?

Henry would soon find out. In the meantime he was in despair about his sons. In Winchester Castle there was a strange wall painting of a huge eagle beset by four little eaglets who were pecking and clawing at the eagle's eyes and wings. Henry explained to a friend that the eagle was himself, the eaglets his sons. He added, "Thus will they pursue me until I die." The devil's streak in Henry was showing more and more in his sons. They continued to plot against their father or to fight among themselves. Young Henry became insanely jealous of Richard, who far surpassed him in skill at arms and military leadership. When King Henry tried to interest the Prince in the arts of ruling—still never giving him any real authority—it was too late. Young Henry was not interested. He wanted the rewards of royalty but none of the hard work his father and mother had so eagerly and ably undertaken. Spoiled and restless, he longed to leave England for the more exciting life in Aquitaine, where tournaments and romance beckoned.

Once back in the turbulent south, he was teased and taunted as the "Lord of little land," a crowned Prince without lands to rule or revenues to collect.

Spoiling for a fight, his friends did their best to inflame him and to stir up his resentment not only against his father, but also against his brothers. When he had squandered all his money, he and some of his disreputable companions went on a plundering spree, looting churches and shrines of gold and silver treasures, terrorizing the countryside. Perhaps he felt this was one way to draw attention to himself. On this, his last, wild adventure he fell ill with dysentery—so often fatal in those days. Soon he lay dying, tended by his faithful friend, William Marshal. He confessed his sins and asked for his father's forgiveness—even the most hardened sinners became humble and contrite when faced with death. Prince Henry also begged his father to show mercy to his mother, held so long in captivity.

A church deacon was sent to Salisbury Castle to break the news to Eleanor, but Eleanor spoke first, saying that she already knew his message—her son was dead. She had had a dream of her fair son lying on a couch, wearing two crowns, one on top of the other. One was his solid gold earthly crown, the other was composed of unearthly light and shone with the brilliance of the Holy Grail. Eleanor explained to the astonished deacon that the crown of celestial light signified everlasting bliss, that her son had been forgiven and had risen to Heaven.

The popular Prince was widely mourned. People forgot his weaknesses and remembered only his beauty, his generosity, and his charm. It was probably due to the Prince's dying request that Eleanor was allowed more freedom for a while. She visited her oldest daughter, Matilda, back from Germany, staying with her all through the winter, and was with her at the birth of a son. At about this time Eleanor received two unexpected gifts from King Henry—a lovely scarlet robe lined with miniver and a saddle trimmed with gold.

Then Henry invited Eleanor to Windsor Castle for Christmas. This was to be both a family gathering and a business meeting to settle once again their sons' inheritance. Prince Henry's sudden death called for a redistribution of lands among their sons. Eleanor was now sixty-two and had been in captivity ten years. Though her hair was graying and her laughing eyes had grown more serious, she was still a lovely woman who moved with grace and dignity. Her mind was as sharp as ever, and she could still exert political influence. Henry had not aged so well, and looked older than his fifty-one years. He had grown stout, and he limped from a wound inflicted by a horse. Always careless of his dress, he had become positively sloppy and unkempt. While Eleanor had become more serene, Henry had become more irascible, often acting more like a suspicious despot than the great ruler he had been. If Henry thought he could use his captive Queen as a political pawn, he soon found out that her punishment had not made her any more docile.

At the Christmas gathering Eleanor realized that Henry expected her to use her influence on Richard, to persuade him to go along with new arrangements for him and his brothers. The King wanted Eleanor to make Richard give up Aquitaine to his little brother John. One can imagine how Eleanor bristled at the idea of giving up Aquitaine, especially to little John, of all her sons the least promising. It was obvious that John had become Henry's favorite as Richard was hers. Both Eleanor and Richard suspected that Henry was laying the groundwork to bypass Richard, now the rightful heir to the English throne, in favor of John. Eleanor began to wonder if those fine presents, the fur-lined cloak and gilded saddle, were just bribes. But gifts or no gifts, she flatly refused to go along with Henry's plans. She pointed out to her husband that Aquitaine was not his to give—that she and Richard held it in their own right, as vassals of the King of France. Eleanor was forceful enough to block Henry's schemes to juggle their sons' inheritance. Not only did Richard and Geoffrey support her stand; the barons at the meeting also backed her. The meeting ended with bitter feelings—the King furious at Eleanor's political triumph and even more hostile to Richard than before.

After this period of relative freedom, it was harder than ever for Eleanor to be sent back to Salisbury Castle to resume the monotony and dreary life of a prisoner. Three months later her son Geoffrey was killed in a tournament. Thrown to the ground, he was trampled to death by galloping horses. Now only two of Eleanor's sons were left: her pride and joy, Richard, and Henry's darling, John. Eleanor

Mail-clad knights in battle.

knew that they would soon be battling for their inheritance.

And battle they did, sometimes against each other, sometimes against their father, and, nearly always, with the aid of the new French King Philip.

Philip was a far cry from his timid father, Louis, and he lacked the charisma of Eleanor's sons. He was not much to look at—untidy in dress, with a shock of unkempt hair and one blind eye. Cold and calculating, he had one ambition: to break asunder the great Plantagenet stranglehold on power and to win back bit by bit the lands he felt belonged to France. What Philip lacked in appeal he made up in cleverness. He knew how to use the weaknesses of others for his own ends. He saw that he could play on Richard's fears that his father meant to displace him with John. After he promised to back Richard, the two became close friends, plotting against King Henry.

In 1187 news from the Holy Land interrupted the schemings and bickerings of the kings and princes of Europe. Jerusalem had been captured by the Moslem Sultan Saladin. The Tomb of Christ and the True Cross, the most sacred of all Christian relics, were now in the hands of the "infidel dogs." The church cried out for a new crusade. Richard immediately signed up; King Henry and King Philip, somewhat reluctantly, soon followed suit. All promised to obey the Truce of God, the church ban on local fighting while men prepared for the crusade.

The Truce of God did not last long. While Henry was in England, gathering men and equipment for the crusade, rebellion broke out again in Normandy. Before crossing the Channel to deal with it, Henry stopped in Salisbury. If he saw Eleanor, it was for the last time. As so often in the past, a storm arose during his Channel crossing, blotting out his island kingdom and his captive Queen in a tempest of wind and rain.

Things were now coming to a showdown between Henry, Philip, and Richard. The crusade had to wait while the Christian kings settled their own petty quarrels. Convinced that his father meant to disinherit him, Richard had joined forces with the wily Philip. Many knights deserted Henry, thinking their future lay with Richard. Only a few friends remained loyal to the old King, now worn out and sick. His leg wound had festered, pain and fever spread through his body. It was clear that he did not have long to live. Despite his illness, he answered a last summons to parley with King Philip and Richard. He was so feeble that he could barely keep his seat astride his horse. Even the ungallant Philip was moved to offer him a cloak to sit on, but the old King scorned the offer. As was his custom, he would parley on horseback. But he was not prepared for Philip's harsh terms—that he give up all his continental lands to Richard and recognize him as heir to the throne of England. An ominous clap of thunder rent the air, Henry reeled in his saddle, but he mustered enough strength to whisper fiercely to his son, "God grant I may not die before I have my revenge on you."

He was carried back to his castle of Chinon, where he soon lay dying. He asked to see the names of those who had deserted him. When he found that his beloved John was one, he turned his face to the wall, saying, "It is enough, I care no more for myself or for the world." And he could be heard muttering, "Shame, shame, shame on a conquered king."

XII

Eleanor and Richard

With Henry gone, no one disputed that Richard was the heir to the English throne. He immediately sent the loyal knight William Marshal to England to free the Queen, but she was already at liberty. Her guards had not dared keep her captive once the news of Henry's death was known. William was amazed to see Eleanor looking so well. She had somehow managed to keep physically and mentally fit all those fifteen long years. She seemed to have stored up her energy rather than lost it, and she emerged from prison a wiser and more understanding woman than she had ever been. She was sixty-seven years old.

No one objected when she assumed the responsibility of governing until Richard could be crowned.

She went first to London and received oaths of allegiance on behalf of her son. Then, in a frankly political move, Eleanor toured England to gain popularity for Richard, so little known to the English. Having experienced how hateful prisons were, Eleanor opened their doors and released prisoners who had languished for a long time waiting for the King's justice. In Richard's name she pardoned many criminals and trespassers against Henry's harsh forest rules—poachers of the royal forests could be punished by mutilation or even death. Her life as a prisoner had somehow taught her compassion for the underprivileged, the poor, and the sick. From a queen of the troubadours who had inspired romance and poetry, she became a queen with as much authority as a king. Her decisions were respected, her concern for her subjects won their affection. Henry had been admired and feared; Eleanor was admired and loved.

She introduced some much-needed reforms, including uniform systems of coins and of weights and measures—coins varied from town to town and the same amount of liquid was called a quart in one place, a pint in another, much to the confusion of buyers and sellers. Eleanor changed all that so that the same coins, the same weights and measures for liquids, for grain, and for cloth, could be used throughout England. Like Henry's legal reforms, these helped to unify the kingdom. Eleanor endeared herself to monasteries and abbeys by relieving them of an annoying, expensive burden—

the care and stabling of the king's horses. Henry had imposed this unpopular duty on monks and abbots so that he could always count on fresh horses whenever he needed them for his speedy trips through the land, or when he had a sudden whim to ride into the forest to hunt wild boar or deer.

Then Eleanor paved the way for an enthusiastic reception of Richard and prepared London for the most splendid coronation it had yet witnessed. She knew that Richard, unlike his father, would enjoy being part of such a magnificent pageant. When Richard arrived in England, preparations were already under way. The streets of London were swept clean and strewn with fresh rushes, house fronts were decorated with banners and tapestries for the procession that wound its way to Westminster Abbey. Passing into the nave of the church came the dignitaries bearing the jeweled crown, the golden spurs, the sword of state, the royal scepters and coronation robes. Then came Richard, walking beneath a silken canopy held aloft by four barons. Eleanor gazed with rapture on her son, who looked every inch a king. Tall and shapely, he had the figure of a warrior knight, and his handsome face with its fine features was framed with amber-gold hair. People thrilled to see he wore the crusader's cross on his royal robe. Before the high altar, lighted by tall tapers, he was anointed with holy oil and crowned by the Archbishop of Canterbury. He then gave his three-fold oath—to uphold the church, to suppress wrongdoing, and to temper justice with mercy. He was proclaimed Richard the First, King of England, and as he took the throne, voices filled the abbey singing the Te Deum.

This great spectacle was almost the last view the English had of their new king. He stayed in England only long enough to raise money for the crusade. He put up for sale everything he could think of—castles, manors, even public offices. "I would sell all London if I could find a buyer," he joked. But even Richard's money raising did not dampen the ardor for the crusade. On both sides of the Channel every town, village, and port was alive with activity. The sound of the forester's axe was heard felling huge oaks for shipbuilding. Ropes were made, sails sewed together. Every forge belched forth black smoke as smiths hammered out horseshoes, links for chain mail, helmets, shields, swords, spears, and bolts for the new, deadly weapon, the crossbow—so deadly that the church had banned its use except against the enemies of Christ. Peasants were busy slaughtering pigs and curing them into great slabs of bacon to be stashed on board ships. Never before had there been such well-thought-out preparations for a crusade. This was to be a strictly military expedition—there would be no women, no troubadours, no rabble of ill-equipped pilgrims tagging along.

Eleanor followed Richard to the continent early in 1190, glad to leave behind the damp and fog of another English winter, to forget those fifteen dreary years in Salisbury. She breathed more freely in her

Crusader ship approaching the Holy Land.

native land. Even her bitterness toward her husband softened. She gave a generous grant to the abbey where he was buried—"For the repose of Henry's soul."

While Richard made his final preparations for the crusade, Eleanor planned for the future. Though a regent had been appointed to rule while her son was overseas, Eleanor knew that Richard put most of his trust in her. In fact she would be the real ruler of the vast Plantagenet realm, from the borders of Scotland to the Pyrenees, while he was on crusade.

Eleanor also had the unpleasant job of keeping close watch on her son John. Though John had inherited the family good looks and quick wit and could be charming at times, he was devious and scheming. As his father's favorite, he had been led to believe that he might be king instead of Richard. Eleanor had to make sure he didn't take advantage of Richard's absence to try to gain the English throne.

The crusading host gathered at Vézelay, where Eleanor had heard Abbot Bernard preach the Second Crusade forty-four years earlier. She would not be going on the great adventure this time, but she could be proud of her son Richard. With his knightly bearing, his courtesy and military prowess, he far outshone King Philip, who was barely able to ride a horse and was known to be a coward in battle. Now that King Henry was dead, Richard and Philip, who had united against the old King when it had served their purpose, began to distrust each other—a bad omen for the joint enterprise.

Eleanor was almost seventy, but she was too busy to feel old. As soon as the crusaders set off, she started on a long journey. She had been concerned that Richard at thirty-three was still unmarried. She felt he must have a wife to provide him with an heir in order to foil any of John's attempts to gain the throne. South of her province of Aquitaine lay the Kingdom of Navarre, whose Princess Berengaria—"a gentle lady, virtuous and fair"—had once met and pleased Richard. With her son's agreement, Eleanor planned to take Berengaria, the bride-to-be, to the island of Sicily, where the crusaders were waiting out the winter before sailing to the Holy Land. Though the approach of wintry weather would have made many a man hesitate to cross the Alps, the courageous old Queen was undaunted. Taking her young charge and a small escort, she set off on horseback through the lower Alps into northern Italy and on down its western coast. The trip took longer than expected, and it was almost Easter by the time they reached the tip of Italy, where one of Richard's ships conveyed them to Sicily. Eleanor's arrival at the crusader camp caused a sensation. Few could believe that the old Queen could make such a trip. "Queen Eleanor, a matchless woman," wrote an admirer, "still indefatigable for every undertaking . . . was the marvel of her age." Unfortunately Eleanor's arrival among the crusaders also touched off the old French antagonism for the Queen. Though they viewed her with a certain awe, the French could not resist recalling her adventures on the Second Crusade, and spreading anew the outworn gossip and ribald tales of her stay in Antioch.

This did not mar Eleanor's joy in seeing her son once more before he set sail. Her only disappointment was to miss the wedding—she had even brought Richard a splendid wedding outfit—since weddings were banned during Lent. Eleanor dared not linger long, lest John cause trouble in her absence. She stayed in Sicily only four days, but during her short visit she saw her daughter, Joanna, Queen of Sicily, for the first time in fifteen years. Since the wedding had to be postponed, Eleanor—disregarding the ban against women on this crusade—arranged to send

Joanna, recently widowed, as chaperone and companion for Berengaria in the Holy Land.

Then Eleanor tore herself away from her two children and once more took the long, difficult trip through Italy and over the Alps. After all her trouble, her hopes of Richard's having an heir were to come to nothing. Though Richard married Berengaria and had her crowned Queen of England, he rarely saw her after that. He had little interest in women and neglected his young bride. Luckily, Berengaria had the companionship of Joanna, who became her closest friend.

Back from her long trip, Eleanor settled down in Normandy, near the Channel, keeping an eye on England as well as the continent. She became Richard's watchdog, seeing that John behaved and that the Truce of God was observed.

People were pleased to have her sign herself "Eleanor, by the Grace of God, Queen of England," though she was really now only the Queen Mother. But everyone looked to her for leadership, marveling at her decisiveness, her fair-mindedness, her unceasing work for the good of the realm. Though John was a problem, spreading evil tales about his absent brother, she managed to keep him in check. Eleanor foresaw that the greatest menace to Richard would be King Philip. She knew enough about him not to trust him. She, as no one else, understood his determination to get revenge for all that his family and his kingdom had suffered from the Plantagenets.

Her fears materialized sooner than she expected. After only six months Philip, pleading sickness, abandoned the crusade and returned home.

Both Philip and Richard had contracted a strange fever, causing their hair and nails to fall out, during their long siege of the enemy seaport Acre. Philip became sick in mind as well as body—his real trouble was jealousy of his more glamorous, fearless companion in arms. At every turn Richard stole the glory, with deeds of valor and chivalry that won him the name of Richard the Lion Heart. The troops adored Richard, and everyone looked to him as the real leader of the crusade. Philip couldn't stand being so overshadowed by his co-leader. Complaining of still being sick, and very angry, he departed for France, but not before Richard extracted his oath to keep the Truce of God.

The Germans, who had been fighting the crusade long before Richard appeared, resented the English King too. When Acre finally fell to the crusaders, Richard arrogantly claimed the victory for the English and set himself up in the royal palace. When he saw the German banner run up next to his, he defiantly had it thrown into a muddy ditch. At this insult many Germans abandoned the crusade, vowing vengeance on the English King. Richard was left to carry on the war by himself.

Now that King Philip was home, Eleanor had to be more vigilant than ever. As she feared, Philip wasted no time in stirring up trouble and intriguing with John against his absent brother. Breaking his oath, Philip invaded Normandy and summoned John from England to join him. John was preparing to cross the Channel with an army, but Eleanor beat him to it. She crossed first in the opposite direction. With a speed worthy of Henry, she dashed to London, Oxford, Windsor, and Winchester to talk to nobles and officers of the crown. Many of them had already given support to John, who had spread lies that Richard would never return, that he planned to remain in the Holy Land for the rest of his life. It took Eleanor's most eloquent pleas, even tears, to persuade the barons to prevent John from leaving England. Her alertness and persuasiveness saved Richard's realm for the moment.

XIII

The Ransom

In the fall of 1192 the Third Crusade was over. It had ended in a stalemate. Richard had gained a few coastal towns, but Jerusalem and the True Cross remained in Moslem hands. The great Moslem leader, Sultan Saladin, however, showed a tolerance unknown to the Christian knights of the West, leaving Jerusalem open to both Moslem and Christian pilgrims.

Much blood had been spilled on the desert sands of the Holy Land; there had been great deeds of bravery and chivalry between the two opponents, Saladin and Richard, who won the admiration of the enemy as well as Christians. But it was high time that Richard, who had been getting urgent

A nineteenth-century artist's interpretation of Richard reluctantly leaving the Holy Land.

letters from his mother, return to see to the safety of his lands.

Through November and December crusaders trickled home. Eleanor heard that Berengaria and Joanna, sent in a separate ship, had landed in Italy, but there was no news of her beloved son. Christmas came and went but still no word. Eleanor was in despair.

Then, shortly after New Year's, 1193, the Queen learned the dreadful news—Richard was a prisoner in Germany. He had been shipwrecked near northern Italy and, while passing through Germany, had been captured and imprisoned. Eleanor, of course, was outraged, but John and Philip, hoping that Richard was as good as dead, immediately plotted to invade England. Once again Eleanor's prompt action foiled them. She ordered all castles to strengthen their garrisons and closed all Channel ports against invasion. She instructed all Englishmen, including peasants, to arm themselves with any weapons available, even pitchforks, in self-defense.

Having checked foul play for a second time, Eleanor dispatched messengers to Germany to find out where Richard was imprisoned. She sent messages to leaders of the Christian world to come to her son's aid. She, who had so recently been a prisoner, could not bear to think of Richard languishing in some remote German stronghold. In her anguish she even wrote to the Pope, scolding him for doing nothing to help her son, the great hero of the Holy

War against the infidels. "The kings and princes of the earth have conspired against my son, the anointed of the Lord. One keeps him in chains while another ravages his lands. . . . Justice, the fear of God, faith and honor have dispersed. Arise, Seigneur, why do you sleep?" She signed herself, with the boldness and indignation that only a distraught mother would dare use, "Eleanor, by the wrath of God, Queen of England."

Finally the Germans agreed to release their distinguished prisoner on the payment of a huge ransom, 150,000 silver marks (some thirty-five tons of silver) and the delivery of 200 hostages. Richard sent his sister, Marie, a poem composed in prison lamenting that his friends did nothing to help him.

No prisoner can tell his honest thought
Unless he speaks as one who suffers wrong;
But for his comfort he may make a song.
My friends are many, but their gifts are
naught.
Shame will be theirs, if, for my ransom, here
I lie another year.

Eleanor received a personal note from her son to his "much-loved mother," asking that she take charge of raising the ransom. She was the only one he trusted. How, she wondered, could she ever raise such a sum from lands that had already been bled dry for the crusade? Whom could she persuade to go as hostages to Germany?

This did not stop her and she went to work to

raise the greatest ransom ever demanded. Though it was the duty of every loyal vassal to contribute to a king's ransom, she knew she could not raise enough that way. She saw that everyone and every institution was taxed; churches and monasteries gave up their gold and silver treasures, even altar crosses. One monastery, lacking gold and silver valuables, gave its year's supply of wool. As the ransom trickled in—far too slowly, it seemed to the impatient Queen—Eleanor placed her seal upon it and stowed it in the crypt of St. Paul's Cathedral for safekeeping.

At the end of a year Eleanor was ready, and set off across the wintry Channel with the heavy chests of ransom silver, accompanied by a group of English nobles. They made their way by road and by river to the valley of the Rhine. Eleanor could hardly wait to see and free her son. But when she reached the city of Mainz, she was stunned by rumors that the German Emperor might change his mind, that he was hesitating about releasing his royal prisoner after all. He had received a message from Philip and John—those evil plotters—that they would match the ransom if the Germans would keep Richard another year! After all Eleanor's ceaseless work, month after month, this was too much. Even the Germans were indignant at the Emperor's behavior. He had given his oath to release Richard upon payment of the ransom, and here it was within his grasp. Was he going to break his oath and stoop to taking a bribe?

An assembly was called to discuss the matter, and Richard was allowed to speak in his own defense. The courtly manners taught him long ago by his mother were useful to him now. He answered all charges against him, many fabricated by King Philip, with such eloquence, such grace and feeling, that he gained the sympathy of the entire gathering. Many were moved to tears. Even the Emperor was moved to change his mind again: He offered to release Richard immediately on condition that the English King pay homage to him for all his lands. Richard bristled at this blow to his pride. Why should he, the great crusader King of England, pay homage to a German Emperor? But Eleanor, whose one concern was to free her son, and fearing that he might display the terrible family temper and undo everything, took Richard aside. She quietly persuaded him that once back in England, the vassal's oath to such a distant ruler would not mean much. So Richard knelt in homage to the Emperor and gained his freedom. Worn out but happy, the old Queen fell weeping into her son's arms. And everyone else wept at the sight of their embrace.

Upon hearing that Richard was free, Philip dispatched a message to John, warning that "the Devil is unchained." Whatever new conspiracy they had been hatching subsided for the moment.

Richard was hailed in England as a conquering hero, the crusader who, deserted by the French and Germans, had checked the foe almost single-handedly. But Eleanor's tact was needed to make sure that all England was loyal to the rightful King, that none of John's followers remained to make trouble. After giving thanks for the King's deliverance at the shrine of St. Thomas at Canterbury and St. Paul's Cathedral, she and Richard went north to Nottingham, the seat of John's rebellion. Having made sure of Nottingham's loyalty, they spent a night at Clipston Castle near Sherwood Forest, the vast royal hunting preserve. According to later ballads, Richard was eager to meet the famous outlaw Robin Hood, who robbed the rich and gave to the poor. Disguised as an abbot, Richard rode into the forest and was halted by Robin Hood. When Richard discovered that Robin Hood was a loyal vassal to the King, he threw off his disguise and joined the outlaw and his merry men in a great feast under the greenwood tree. Whether the tale is true or not, Eleanor's recently relaxed forest rules might well have enabled outlaws to hide out in the depths of Sherwood's dense forest.

After this trip Eleanor staged a second coronation for her son, to restore his royal dignity and wipe out his humiliating oath of allegiance to the Emperor. On a dais set up in the transept of the church, Eleanor shared the glory of this occasion equally with her son. To the English the courageous old Queen Mother was still the Queen of England. No one seemed to notice the absence of Richard's wife, the real Queen, Berengaria, who was touring Italy with Joanna. Soon after the coronation Eleanor and Richard left for the continent. They would not return—in Richard's ten-year reign, he spent only six months in England.

In Normandy John appeared, humble and full of remorse. Fearing his brother, he sought Eleanor first, that she might intercede in his behalf. Acting on the advice of his mother, who thought it wise to keep John on their side, Richard was generous to the young brother who had betrayed him, saying, "John mistakes me if he is afraid. After all, he is my brother." For the moment the fickle John agreed to support Richard against King Philip.

Eleanor was tired now, and decided to retire to the Abbey of Fontevrault where Henry had once wanted to set her up as abbess. But Eleanor came to Fontevrault as neither nun nor abbess, but as a royal visitor to its luxurious guest house. This abbey was a complex of lovely Romanesque buildings near the Loire River. It had all the charm of a vast country estate, yet it was not far from the crossroads of traffic. Eleanor could rest here, but she could also easily get news of what was going on.

The news was not good, and Eleanor did not rest easily. Fighting between Richard and Philip began in earnest. Interspersed with truces, the war dragged on for five years. Both Kings were using hired mercenaries. Eleanor worried that if Philip had more of them, Richard's superior courage and skill might not count. She remembered how Henry had shocked Aquitaine by his use of mercenaries, hated for their ferocity and lack of chivalry. But things were changing—there was that new lethal crossbow that Richard swore by. So many things had changed in Eleanor's long life, even warfare. War seemed more deadly now, less glorious.

To protect the northern borders of his Duchy of Normandy, Richard built an extraordinary castle on a rocky summit, high above the Seine River. With its rounded contours, it seemed to flow right out of its rocky foundation. Eleanor had not seen it, but she heard that it surpassed all other castles in Europe in design, strength, and beauty. She was proud to learn that Richard had designed it himself. With its round towers, instead of square ones, it was a new step in castle architecture. Richard named it Château Gaillard—Saucy Castle—in defiance of the French.

During a truce in 1199, which both Kings used to raise more money and men, Richard visited his mother in Fontevrault. While discussing his desperate need for funds, he heard a strange tale—that a vast treasure of buried gold had been found near the small castle of Châlus. This seemed a fairy-tale answer to his needs. Richard hastened to lay hold of it. The owner of the castle fled at the King's approach, leaving only a handful of knights and peasants on guard. As the King reconnoitered the castle grounds, he noticed a young man standing on the parapet holding a frying pan for a shield in one hand and a crossbow in the other. Suddenly a bolt whizzed through the air and struck the unarmed King below the nape of his neck, near his spine. Back in his tent Richard tried to pull out the bolt, but the shaft broke off, leaving the iron barb deeply imbedded in his flesh. A barber-surgeon was called in. By the light of a lantern he brutally hacked away the flesh and finally dug out the barb. Though ointments were applied, the wound swelled and turned black. Gangrene set in within a few days. Richard knew he could not survive and sent for his mother. Traveling day and night from Fontevrault, a hundred miles to the north, Eleanor "came like the wind," and was at her son's side before he died.

Richard named his brother John as his heir. He then asked to see the man who had shot him. "What harm have I done you that you have killed me?" asked Richard.

"You once slew my father and my brother. Take what revenge you like," answered the peasant.

"Go in peace," said Richard. "I forgive you my death and will exact no revenge." The man was unshackled and Richard gave him a gift in token of his full mercy, his last chivalrous act.

Richard died in his mother's arms. The grief-stricken Queen felt that she had lost the "staff of her age, the light of her eyes." Of all her sons, Richard had been the most promising, the most talented. He had been closest to her and had fulfilled her ideals of knighthood—a fearless warrior, a courteous knight, and beneath his chain mail a poet and artist too. As with his brother Prince Henry, his faults—his terrible temper, his arrogance, and his greed—would be forgotten. His daring exploits and chivalrous deeds proclaimed him one of the greatest knights of the Middle Ages. Eleanor accompanied the slow-moving funeral cortege back to Fontevrault, where Richard, according to his own request, was buried at the feet of his father. But parts of him were buried elsewhere according to the royal custom—his heart encased in a gilded casket was sent to a cathedral in Normandy, his entrails to Poitou. As Eleanor gazed at her handsome son, dressed for burial in his coronation finery, velvet robes, jeweled gloves, and golden sandals, it must have seemed a cruel turn of fate that, of all her five sons, only John Lackland, the worst of the lot, remained.

XIV

Eleanor and John

In the midst of her sorrow Eleanor was faced with the most difficult political crisis of her life—to supporting and helping her unreliable and unpopular son John to take Richard's place as King of England, ruler of Normandy, Anjou, and Aquitaine. To try to mold John, noted for his treachery and evil acts, into a kingly character was challenge enough, but even more difficult would be keeping King Philip from snatching the Plantagenet lands from her weak son.

She would have to act quickly, for there was another claimant to the English throne. Some people thought her little grandson Arthur of Brittany, son of her dead older son Geoffrey, had a better claim. But there was little to recommend Arthur, only a powerless twelve-year-old, except the magic of his name, and Eleanor despised Arthur's mother, Constance, as much as Constance despised Eleanor, her mother-in-law, and all the Plantagenets. But the worst thing about Arthur was that he was already in the clutches of the crafty King Philip. Philip had taken the fatherless boy to Paris, where he was schooling him to hate his uncle John and all his Plantagenet relatives and leading Arthur to think he was the rightful heir to all their lands. Arthur was too young to realize that Philip was only using him for his own ends—to break the Plantagenet power. Eleanor could see that backing Arthur would simply be playing into the enemy's hands. John, a grown man, seemed the lesser of two evils. In any case Richard had named him as his heir. That was enough for Eleanor—and for the faithful William Marshal, who set off to England to prepare John's coronation.

Eleanor was now seventy-seven, but she didn't let her age or her sorrow hold her back. After making gifts to the Abbey of Fontevrault "for the repose of my very dear lord, King Richard," and gifts to his trusted friends and servants—a bake house to one, a manor to his old governess, even a village to his valet—she was off on another political goodwill tour of Aquitaine to prepare it for the future. Through her generosity and understanding, she hoped to gain its lasting loyalty to her and its future Duke, the new King John of England. She knew she could get better support for him without his presence. She went alone.

It had been a long time since she had made a

thorough tour of her own duchy, and she noticed many changes—roads were better, the land seemed more lush and cultivated than ever, towns had grown bigger, new ones had sprung up. There was an air of prosperity despite some areas devastated by Richard and Philip's recent battles. As a young Queen Eleanor had never thought how the poor peasants and village folk suffered from warring knights who trampled their farms, burned their villages, and mercilessly killed anyone in their way. To the thoughtless nobles war was a game. After flying at each other's throats, they often became friends again, wining and dining together, while the poor peasants either were dead or had lost everything. More than ever before, Eleanor saw the need for peace.

She talked to merchants and artisans in the towns and, at their request, granted charters giving the towns freedom to run their own governments. Some of her charters freed the townspeople from irksome obligations to their local overlords—from bridge tolls, demands for military service, and yearly gifts of their labor. But in return for these privileges, they would be responsible for defending their own towns.

In Poitiers, which sixty years earlier she and Louis had punished so severely for daring to ask for freedom, she now granted a charter, which gave it that freedom. She also granted families the right to choose husbands for their daughters without their lord's consent. The charter further specified that no citizen could be imprisoned except for murder, theft, or treachery. Eleanor may not have fully realized the benefit of her charters—that free citizens would take more pride in improving and defending their towns, in maintaining order and increasing trade. Even though Eleanor had reached an age when many people tend to live in the past and to resist change, she was on the wave of the future. Kings would follow her example, seeing the advantage of granting freedom to towns in exchange for their support and thus binding them more directly to the monarchy.

Eleanor's trip took her as far south as Bordeaux, west to the Atlantic coast, and back north to the Loire valley—almost a thousand miles in three months of summer heat. Henry could hardly have done better.

Reassured of Aquitaine's support by the success of her trip, Eleanor decided to fulfill a humiliating obligation in the further interest of peace—to pay homage to her overlord, King Philip, for all her lands. She knew the value of a vassal's oath. But it was especially odious to Eleanor to pay homage to the man who had deserted her son Richard on crusade, then plotted with John against him, and was even now plotting with her grandson Arthur against the new King John and herself. But swallowing her pride, she knelt before King Philip—young enough to be her son—and placed her old hands in his, giving him her vassal's oath of allegiance. Philip's one eye looked coldly at her as he gave her the customary kiss of peace, hateful to them both. By this act Eleanor was once more recognized as Duchess of Aquitaine, its rightful ruler until she died, and the King was obliged to protect her, his vassal. She hoped that this gesture of peace would curb any schemes Philip might be hatching with Arthur to seize her lands south of the Loire River.

Shortly after this and only five months after Richard's death, Eleanor had another sorrow when her youngest daughter, Joanna, died. Her oldest daughter, Marie, had died the year before, Alix the year before that, and Matilda some ten years earlier. Of her ten children, only two remained: John and her namesake Eleanor, Queen of faraway Castile, in Spain.

Eleanor never seemed to have time to indulge her sorrows. Once more she was on the road, on one more errand of peace—to carry out a marriage contract between a granddaughter and the new French Prince. Her granddaughter would be marrying the grandson of her ex-husband, Louis. Whatever Eleanor thought of this combination, she hoped it would cement the new peace treaty between John and Philip. In early January of the year 1200, the dawn of a new century, Eleanor, now seventy-eight, set off with her escort along the pilgrim highway heading south to the pass of Roncesvalles, which led over the Pyrenees Mountains to Spain. Winter winds and sleet made the going difficult, but at the head of the pass was a welcome monastery where pilgrims and travelers found bed and rest. As they came down the pass, the mists lifted and the foothills of the Pyrenees opened to a welcoming plain where the going was easier. The mountains behind them now sparkled in Spain's brilliant sunshine.

By the end of January Eleanor arrived in Castile,

where her daughter presided over a court as refined and cultivated as her own had been in Poitiers. Eleanor found her beautiful daughter, whom she had not seen for thirty years, surrounded by her eleven children. Eleanor was asked to choose among her eligible granddaughters the one she thought most suited to be the future Queen of France. She chose twelve-year-old Blanche, in whom she sensed a strong, queenly character much like her own. Eleanor chose well—Blanche would prove to be a great queen of France and the mother of a great French king and saint, Louis IX.

Eleanor stayed in Castile for two months, delighting in her family and feeling happily remote from the political controversy up north. Pleasant memories of her youth and her former court at Poitiers revived as she listened to troubadours sing of love, heard seductive Spanish music, and watched young couples dance the fandango.

Then Eleanor and her granddaughter set off for the north, crossing the Pyrenees in the first flush of spring. The going was slow, as the roads were crowded with pilgrims heading toward their favorite shrines for Easter. They stopped in Bordeaux and stayed in Eleanor's old ducal palace. From a balcony Eleanor could point out to Blanche the meadow across the river where Prince Louis and the French had pitched their tents when they had come sixty-three years before to fetch her as a bride. Few grandmothers had as much to tell a granddaughter as Eleanor, whose life had been so packed full of adventure.

Thirteenth-century carved wooden bridal box. Two musicians play for the couple in the center.

Eleanor and her granddaughter parted company in Fontevrault, the old Queen returning there to rest once more while little Blanche went north to meet her unknown future husband. No doubt Eleanor warned her granddaughter that she would find the ways of Paris different from those of Castile. Eleanor now felt she had done all she could in the interests of peace and saving the Plantagenet realm. Though growing feebler, Eleanor was not idle. She continued to communicate with John, giving him valuable diplomatic advice—to which he sometimes paid attention.

XV

Eleanor's Last Adventure

The peace for which Eleanor had worked so hard came abruptly to an end in 1202. John's devious behavior undid it all when he underhandedly snatched away a bride-to-be from a prominent noble and married her himself. The noble complained to his overlord, King Philip, who summoned John to appear in court. When John refused, Philip declared all John's continental lands forfeit and renewed the war. Now the moment had come for Philip to make use of Eleanor's grandson Arthur. After knighting the young boy and filling him full of glories to come, he sent him swaggering south to take over the Plantagenet lands below the Loire River while he himself invaded Normandy.

When Eleanor heard that Arthur, with two hundred of Philip's handpicked knights, was at the Loire River, only a few miles north of Fontevrault, she reacted with alarm. Were they going to strike at her lands? Did Philip no longer honor her vassal's oath? Did they think she was too old to care? Perhaps they thought she was already dead. They were quite wrong. While there was still breath in her body, she would defend her lands. She somehow found energy to muster an escort and quickly took off for Poitiers, where she had plenty of loyal vassals to help defend her duchy. Eleanor, now over eighty, could no longer travel at her usual speed, and she found the road already blocked by Arthur's knights before she got to Poitiers. She barely had time to detour to the castle of Mirabeau, where she and her own few knights shut themselves up in the central tower and lowered the portcullis. They were not completely secure—the walled town surrounding the castle was poorly protected and there were few provisions to withstand a long siege. Eleanor immediately sent a messenger through the postern gate to her son John, eighty miles away.

When Arthur and his knights discovered Eleanor's whereabouts, they realized that this was an opportunity not to be missed. The risks were little, the stakes were high. Their plan was to lay siege to the castle of Mirabeau, capture the Queen, and hold her for high ransom. With such a hostage they could force John to yield anything they wanted, even Aquitaine. Within three days they had secured the

French medieval walled town with its crenellated tower keep (center).

town below the castle and walled up all the gates except one, which they left open for expected reinforcements. Then the insolent young Arthur began to bargain with his grandmother, offering her freedom in exchange for all her lands. From a tower window, Eleanor played for time, artfully stringing out conversations as long as she could, hoping that her message had reached John and that he was on his way to her rescue. That evening, as darkness was falling, Arthur and his knights conferred. Sure of their quarry, they decided to wait until morning to assault the tower and capture the Queen. It was a balmy, starry July night and the besiegers removed their armor. Most of them fell asleep in the town's streets.

As soon as John had gotten the news of his mother's plight, he had started to her rescue. Aided by the brightness of the stars and moon, he continued to ride at breakneck speed all through the night. He arrived at Mirabeau just before dawn. With swords drawn he and his knights rushed in through the one open gate and fell upon the sleeping French. Those who tried to resist were slain, the others were captured, none escaped.

Then John, with a lack of chivalry that would have horrified his brother Richard, subjected his captured nobles to the most humiliating disgrace—chaining them to oxcarts and parading them through their own estates before depositing them in dungeons. His nephew Arthur, a traitor to the Plantagenets, was thrown into the thick-walled dungeon of Falaise, near the English Channel. He was never seen again. Dark rumors later spread that John had murdered him.

King Philip was beside himself with anger upon hearing that his best knights and Arthur, his instrument to destroy John, had been captured and were languishing in prison. The utter stupidity of it all—just to capture an old Queen who would soon be dead.

This was Eleanor's last and most unusual adventure. Who ever heard of an eighty-year-old grandmother besieged by her own grandson? It had been a close call. Her presence of mind and John's unusually prompt action had saved her. It had been a great victory for John to capture Philip's best knights, but it was his one and only victory over the French.

Once freed, Eleanor continued to Poitiers; but her favorite ancestral castle was small comfort to her. Her great hall, which had once swayed to lively dances and echoed to the songs of troubadours, was ghostly now. It had become what it is called today, "the hall of the lost footsteps." Worn out and sick, Eleanor retired once more to the Abbey of Fontevrault—this time to the care of the nuns.

Soon Eleanor lay dying, and her world seemed to be dying with her. The great empire she had helped to build was disintegrating rapidly. She had done her best to make John into a king, but she could not remake his unstable character, sometimes capable, more often weak and cruel. Without her guidance John let power slip away to the dogged Philip, who was gaining inch by inch, fulfilling the prophecy that he would be a Hammer to the English. But all that became remote to Eleanor when she slipped into a coma. She was probably spared the news that Richard's great rock castle, Château Gaillard, fell to the French after a six-month siege. That meant the loss of Normandy and Anjou, but most of Aquitaine would remain in Plantagenet hands for another two hundred years, as though loyal to its former Duchess.

In Fontevrault the trees were growing green, tiny buds of broom plant—*planta genista*—would soon be bursting into yellow blossoms. Spring had come when Eleanor died on April 1, in the year 1204. She was eighty-two years old and had reigned for sixty-seven years. First Queen of France, then Queen of England, she is most remembered as Eleanor of Aquitaine, Queen of the Troubadours.

She was buried in the abbey church of Fontevrault next to her beloved son Richard and Henry, whom she had once loved so passionately. You can see her effigy still. Her face with its fine features radiates an ageless beauty and intelligence, and there is a faint suggestion of a smile. She holds an open book in her delicate hands. No one knows whether it is a book of prayer or a book of songs.

Amid the crashing of castle walls, as fortress after fortress was falling to the French, little attention was paid to the death of the great Queen. But the nuns who knew her best in her last days wrote, "She enhanced the grandeur of her birth by the honesty of her life. . . . She surpassed almost all the queens of the world."

They might have said much more about this remarkable woman whose life had spanned almost a century, outliving two husbands and all but two of her ten children. From a frivolous, willful young girl she had matured into a wise, understanding woman and a great ruler. She lived life to the full,

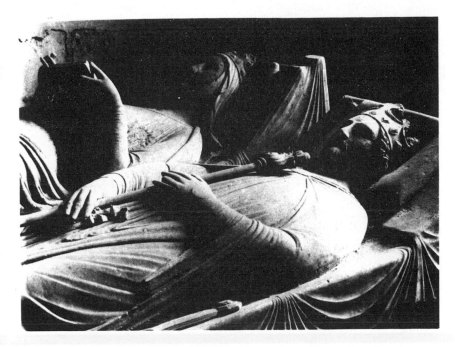

Effigies of Eleanor and Richard in the abbey church of Fontevrault.

facing sorrows and dangers with amazing courage—whether suffering unspeakable hardships in the wild mountains en route to the Holy Land, storm tossed on the high seas, riding over the wintry Alps at the age of seventy, enduring fifteen years of captivity, or daring to express her independence as a woman. Above all she inspired poets to compose beautiful love lyrics and helped to launch a new romantic literature that we still enjoy today.

Though the French would not forgive Eleanor for her marriage to the English King Henry and the loss of Aquitaine, they could not forget her. Her life provided material for balladeers and songsters; they depicted her as siren, sorceress, or fairy queen who could change herself into a demon. They raked up all the unsavory gossip of her behavior including, two centuries after Eleanor's death, the ridiculous story of the Queen offering Fair Rosamond a choice between poison or the dagger. Such was the stuff of ballads. But Eleanor had no need for fantasy or myth to keep her image alive. Her real life was extraordinary enough.

Author's Note

All accounts of Eleanor, whether from admirers or critics, speak of her extraordinary, radiant beauty, but none of them tells us exactly what she looked like. We know her eyes were fascinating but we don't know what color they were. We don't know if she was a blonde or brunette. The ideal beauty of the twelfth century was fair haired and blue eyed, as depicted in all the romances. If Eleanor was a model in looks as well as character for Guinevere and possibly Isolde, she would have been a blonde. Yet she was born in an area where most people were dark haired and brown eyed. I think of Eleanor as having dark, luxuriant hair, high color, and sparkling eyes, but I would not be able to say what color they were.

But whatever Eleanor's type of beauty, she was, as one contemporary said, "a woman beyond compare."

Eleanor of Aquitaine
A Chronology of Her Life

1122   Eleanor born in Bordeaux, Aquitaine.

1137   Eleanor inherits Duchy of Aquitaine, becomes its Duchess. Marries French Prince Louis. They are crowned King and Queen of France.

1144   Dedication of abbey church of St. Denis, first Gothic building.

1145   Eleanor has daughter, Marie, first of ten children.

1147   Eleanor joins Louis on the Second Crusade to rescue the Holy Land from the Moslem Turks. Eleanor quarrels with Louis.

1151   Eleanor meets Duke Henry of Normandy.

1152   Eleanor and Louis divorced.
Eleanor marries Duke Henry.

1153   Birth of William, first of Eleanor's five sons by Henry.

1154   Henry and Eleanor crowned King and Queen of England. They rule from the borders of Scotland to the borders of Spain.

1162   Henry appoints Thomas Becket Archbishop of Canterbury.

1165   Birth of Prince Philip, first and only son of Louis.

1166   Birth of Eleanor's last child, John Lackland.
Rift between Eleanor and Henry. Henry's love affair with Fair Rosamond.

1170   Murder of Thomas Becket in Canterbury Cathedral. Eleanor sets up Courts of Love in Poitiers.

1173   Backed by Eleanor, her sons lead rebellion against King Henry.

1174   Henry imprisons Eleanor in Salisbury Castle, England.

1189   Henry dies, Eleanor freed.
Her favorite son, Richard, crowned King of England.

1190   King Richard and King Philip lead the Third Crusade to capture Jerusalem from the Sultan Saladin.

1192   End of crusade. Richard captured and imprisoned by Germans on way home.

1194   Eleanor ransoms Richard. Has him recrowned King of England.

1195   War between Richard and Philip.

1199   Richard dies of arrow wound. John crowned King of England.

1200   Eleanor crosses Pyrenees at age of seventy-eight to choose granddaughter to marry new French Prince.

1202   Eleanor besieged in castle by grandson, Arthur.

1204   Philip captures Normandy from John. Eleanor dies at age of eighty-two, after reigns spanning sixty-seven years.

ELEANOR'S TEN CHILDREN:

By Louis,   Marie, born 1145, died 1198
Alix, born 1150, died 1197

By Henry,   William, born 1153, died 1156
Henry, born 1155, died in 1183
Matilda (Mother of German Emperor Otto IV), born 1156, died 1189
Richard, born 1157, died 1199
Geoffrey, born 1158, died 1186
Eleanor (Mother of Blanche, grandmother of King Louis IX, Saint), born 1161, died 1214
Joanna, born 1165, died 1199
John, born 1166, died 1216.

For Further Reading

Brooks, Polly Schoyer, and Nancy Zinsser Walworth. *The World of Walls: The Middle Ages in Western Europe*. New York: J.B. Lippincott, 1966.

Duggan, Alfred. *Growing Up in the Thirteenth Century*. New York: Pantheon Books, Inc., 1962.

———. *The Story of the Crusades, 1097–1291*. New York: Pantheon Books, Inc., 1964.

Fremantle, Ann, and the Editors of Time-Life Books. *The Age of Faith*. New York: Time-Life Books, a Division of Time Inc., 1965.

Hartman, Gertrude. *Medieval Days and Ways*. New York: Macmillan Publishing Co., Inc., 1937.

Holmes, Urban T., Jr. *Daily Living in the Twelfth Century*. Madison, Wisc.: University of Wisconsin Press, 1952.

Kelly, Amy. *Eleanor of Aquitaine and the Four Kings*. Cambridge, Mass.: Harvard University Press, 1950.

Konigsburg, E. L. *A Proud Taste for Scarlet and Miniver.* New York: Atheneum, 1973.

Lofts, Norah. *Eleanor the Queen.* New York: Fawcett Crest Books, 1977.

Marks, Claude. *Pilgrims, Heretics and Lovers: A Medieval Journey.* New York: Macmillan Publishing Co., Inc., 1975.

National Geographic Society, eds. *The Age of Chivalry.* Washington, D.C.: National Geographic Society, 1969.

Painter, Sidney. *French Chivalry.* Ithaca, N.Y.: Cornell University Press, 1957.

Power, Eileen. *Medieval People.* New York: Barnes & Noble, Inc., 1963.

———and M. Poston. *Medieval Women.* New York: Cambridge University Press, 1976.

Thomas of Britain. *The Romance of Tristram and Ysolt.* Trans. Roger S. Loomis. Repr. of 1951 ed. New York: Octagon Books.

Trevor-Roper, Hugh R. *The Rise of Christian Europe.* New York: Harcourt, Brace & World, 1965.

White, Freda. *The Ways of Aquitaine.* London: Faber & Faber, Ltd., 1968.

Williams, Jay. *Knights of the Crusades.* New York: Horizon Caravel Books, Harper & Row, Publishers, 1965.

Index